My dear friend John Woodbridge has hooked up with one of the ablest young minds in the Christian world to produce a timely reminder of the great moments in the history of our faith. We live in immensely serious times, and this book is a serious response that could truly inspire the church to do what it must do in our world today. May God use this to light a fire among his people.

—CHUCK COLSON, founder, Prison Fellowship and the Colson Center for Christian Worldview

This book shows how God has moved in extraordinary ways throughout the history of the church. Genuine revival is not the result of marketing, technique, or entrepreneurship. As the stories here show, true revival comes as a "surprising work of God." When this happens, lives are changed, the church reformed, and the world renewed. How we need such a stirring today!

—TIMOTHY GEORGE, founding dean, Beeson Divinity School; general editor, *The Reformation Commentary on Scripture*

Collin Hansen and John Woodbridge write very much in the spirit of Jonathan Edwards in narrating revivals as a means of edifying and inspiring. *A God-Sized Vision* provides accessible and thoughtful accounts of classic American revivals from Edwards to Billy Graham and includes important stories of how in the twentieth-century revivals become some of the most remarkable developments worldwide.

—GEORGE MARSDEN, author, *Jonathan Edwards: A Life* and *A Shorter Life of Jonathan Edwards*

How soon we forget! While we must never despise the ordinary means of grace that God customarily uses in the salvation of men and women, we must not forget those extraordinary times when in his mercy God has seemed to come down and pour out his Spirit in such transforming power that all of our expectations are reduced to rubble in the sheer glory of the transforming presence of God. Yes, many of these movements had downsides and charlatans connected with them— but fair-minded assessment must stand in grateful awe for these "visitations." May the renewed knowledge of what God has done in the past incite us to prayer that God would do it again.

—D. A. CARSON, Research Professor of New Testament, Trinity Evangelical Divinity School

Collin Hansen and John Woodbridge do a remarkable job of summarizing the Spirit-wrought revivals of times past, and then challenging us to pray expectantly for the Holy Spirit to do a similar work in our day. There is no doubt that we desperately need such a ministry of the Spirit. I wish every pastor and Christian leader in America would read this book and begin to pray earnestly for authentic revival in our time.

—JERRY BRIDGES

The authors have done a great service to the body of Christ by providing this treatment of the biblical moorings and patterns for revival and by chronicling some of those divine moments of the past when God pulled back the curtain and manifested his presence in an extraordinary way. This book will leave you longing for such a visitation of his Spirit in our day and praying, "Lord, do it again!"
—NANCY LEIGH DEMOSS, author, *Revive Our Hearts* radio host

Hansen and Woodbridge have given us a rare book on revival. They affirm the supernatural, without being sensationalistic. They celebrate the surprising work of God, without downplaying the ordinary. They demonstrate the ecumenical scope of revival, without ignoring the important role theology plays in the ongoing health of the church. This book will guard us against complacency, cynicism, and, just as importantly, the naiveté that thinks revival solves everything. An encouraging, judicious, well-told tale of God's amazing work around the globe throughout the ages.
—KEVIN DEYOUNG

While reading [*A God-Sized Vision*], I had to stop often to reflect and pray for God to deal with areas in my life that needed his sanctifying, forgiving, and healing grace. God reminded me that those who pray for revival must first pray for revival in their own lives.... May this book challenge Christians to yearn for and pray for the church to experience all that God wishes for it.
—AJITH FERNANDO, national director, Youth for Christ

If ever the world needed the church to be revived, it's now. For, the world doesn't need our savvy programs; it needs God's sovereign power. I pray that this stimulating study of revival and those that God has used to bring revival about will indeed stretch and stir the twenty-first century church to realize once again that the ultimate factor in the church's engagement with society is the church's engagement with God.
—TULLIAN TCHIVIDJIAN, pastor, Coral Ridge Presbyterian Church; author, *Unfashionable: Making a Difference in the World by Being Different*

Compacted in this volume are accounts of the awe-inspiring work of God when he moves upon his people in revival power. The story is told by careful scholars who have a gift for making history come alive. Reading the book will lift one to noble thoughts and dreams of greater things. Take it as a rejuvenating vitamin for your soul.
—ROBERT E. COLEMAN, Distinguished Professor of Evangelism and Discipleship, Gordon-Conwell Theological Seminary

COLLIN HANSEN AND JOHN WOODBRIDGE

A GOD-SIZED VISION

REVIVAL STORIES THAT STRETCH AND STIR

ZONDERVAN®

ZONDERVAN.com/
AUTHORTRACKER
follow your favorite authors

We want to hear from you. Please send your comments about this book to us in care of zreview@zondervan.com. Thank you.

ZONDERVAN

A God-Sized Vision
Copyright © 2010 by Collin Hansen and John Woodbridge

This title is also available as a Zondervan ebook. Visit www.zondervan.com/ebooks.

This title is also available in a Zondervan audio edition. Visit www.zondervan.fm.

Requests for information should be addressed to:

Zondervan, *Grand Rapids, Michigan 49530*

Library of Congress Cataloging-in-Publication Data

Hansen, Collin, 1981–
    A God-sized vision : revival stories that stretch and stir / Collin Hansen and John Woodbridge.
       p. cm.
    Includes bibliographical references and index.
    ISBN 978-0-310-32703-5 (hardcover, jacketed)
    1. Revivals — History. I. Woodbridge, John D., 1941– II. Title.
BV3770.H26 2010
269'.2409 — dc22   2010019074

Cover design: *Micah Kandros*
Cover photography or illustration: *Bridgeman Art Library; Jessica Rinaldi/Reuters/ Corbis; Hulton-Deutsch Collection/Corbis*
Interior design: *Sherri L. Hoffman*
Editorial Assistant: *Emma Sleeth*

Printed in the United States of America

12 13 14 15 /DCI/ 22 21 20 19 18 17 16 15 14 13 12 11 10 9 8 7 6 5 4

To the men and women
throughout the ages
who trusted the heavenly Father
to exalt his Son, Jesus Christ,
by reviving his church
through the power of the Holy Spirit

CONTENTS

PREFACE

What is the problem with revival today? For one thing, few of us living in the West today have ever seen one. Many of those who think they have seen a revival may have in mind events that would not pass the biblical or historical standard. Perhaps their church holds regular "revival" meetings on certain nights of the week or during a summer month. But manipulative appeals to renew your vows to Christ do not constitute revival. During genuine revival, the Holy Spirit contends and convicts, but he does not manipulate as he grants Christians a new experience of God's presence and power.

Others who claim to know about revival can tell you all about the Holy Spirit's power. They have flocked to see hundreds healed from every disease known to humankind—and then some. On occasion, however, they seem to have forgotten the Holy Spirit's purpose. Sent by God, the Holy Spirit testifies to the work and words of Jesus Christ (John 14:26). When the Holy Spirit fell on Pentecost, fulfilling the prophecy of Joel 2, the apostle Peter stepped forward to explain that the crucified Jesus was Lord and Christ (Acts 2:36). In revival, Jesus is praised by those who have been saved from sin by his atoning work on the Cross and triumph over death in the Resurrection.

Still others who believe in the miracles nevertheless function as modern naturalists, limiting their expectations for God's work within the man-made confines of observable, repeatable phenomena. While acknowledging miracles in the Gospels and book of

Acts, some will argue that the Epistles seem more concerned with the ordinary Christian life and struggles with heterodoxy and sin. Seeking revival, these Christians warn, will distract us from appreciating how God works in our midst each day. That he would condescend to us is a miracle in itself. Besides, they argue, revivals flame out quickly. They leave uncertain lasting effects as proponents grow discouraged and critics grow emboldened.

As you can see, the reasons for rejecting revival mount quickly. Some have merit. Indeed, we should never demean God's work, however ordinary. For with the Lord, even the seemingly ordinary is extraordinary grace shown to undeserving sinners. Yet we submit that many Christians have grown so content with the ordinary that they don't bother asking God for anything more. False biblical dichotomies that widen the chasm between the New Testament and us cannot justify reluctance to pray as Jesus and the apostles prayed. We who live in an era of small things must remember eras when the big things seen and heard in the Bible returned once more.

This book is not for those who have grown comfortable with the Christian life. Others, however, will feel the Spirit nudging them toward something more. They will begin to see ways they have been satiated by small things and lost the taste for big things. They may realize that if Jesus is truly Lord, then everything changes. The timeworn routines that promise peace no longer satisfy. They will embrace a God-sized vision for his work in this world. We cannot pretend that we can see things perfectly from God's perspective. But we can plead with him to give us a glimpse of the world from a loftier vantage point. Few of us are tempted today to dream too big. Rather, our vision shrinks to the size of our limited experience. Yet all things are possible for those who believe in the God who created the heavens and the earth. In our disbelief, we can ask God for inspiration to believe. Then he may give us a vision of divine size.

Martyn Lloyd-Jones saw that vision. He read about revival, taught about it, advocated for it, and prayed fervently to see it. Revival was central to his ministry. "I do not understand Christian people who are not thrilled by the whole idea of revival," said Lloyd-Jones, pastor of Westminster Chapel in London, where he served from 1938 to 1968. "If there is one respect in which God confounds the wisdom of the wise more than in any other it is revival."[1]

Still, Lloyd-Jones never experienced a new chapter in the history of revivals, despite his native Wales's traditional reputation for spawning them. In fact, Lloyd-Jones even failed to reverse the trend of discrediting revivals, a trend that he traced back to 1860. He identified several reasons why Christians no longer think of revival when they lament a world that does not know Christ. Conservatives would rather work to reform church theology and practice. Intellectuals doubt supernatural intervention. Rationalists dismiss emotional enthusiasm. All convene committees and organize campaigns. But few will plead for revival, Lloyd-Jones argued. And yet revival didn't come. Should we conclude, then, that Lloyd-Jones was wrong to place such an emphasis on revival?

Surely not, because even though Lloyd-Jones never saw revival, his ministry thrived as he allowed God to expand his vision. He

Revival was central to the ministry of London pastor Martyn Lloyd-Jones. (Photo courtesy of the D. M. Lloyd-Jones Recordings Trust.)

struck the right balance between pleading for God to do what only he can do and striving in the meantime to bolster the church as a faithful minister of the gospel. He was not preoccupied with the spectacular to the point that he neglected gradual gains. Before revival, Lloyd-Jones observed, the church rediscovers the "grand, glorious, central truths" of Scripture.[2] These include justification by faith alone, the authority of Scripture, the substitutionary death of Jesus Christ by his blood on the Cross, his miraculous resurrection, God's sovereign intervention in this world, and judgment for sin. He lived through decades when church leaders gradually drifted from orthodoxy by hedging on these beliefs. Lloyd-Jones feared that evangelicals would be too easily pleased with their apologetic efforts and incremental recovery. But the modern crisis demands a God-sized response.

"However great a defender of the faith he may be, however doughty a champion of orthodoxy, he can fight and sweat and pray and write and do all things, but he is of no avail, he is impotent, he cannot stem the tide," Lloyd-Jones said. "We persist in thinking that we can set the situation right. We start a new society, we write a book, we organize a campaign, and we are convinced that we are going to hold back the tide. But we cannot. When the enemy comes in like a flood, it is the Lord who will raise, and does raise the banner. The fact of revival proves, I say, so clearly again and again the impotence and smallness of man left to himself."[3]

Like the Israelites of old, we so quickly forget what God has done. When we forget, we're tempted to turn against the God who miraculously delivered us from sin and death, as he delivered the Israelites from the pursuing Egyptians who had enslaved them. But our problem today may be worse than mere forgetfulness. We've never even heard many of the revival stories that buoyed the faith of Lloyd-Jones. They've been lost. As the Book of the Law was rediscovered in the days of the Jewish king Josiah (2 Kings 22–23), we need to recover these testimonies of God's faithfulness. Already too many generations have been cut off from their legacy. Sadly, few of us understand the gravity of this challenge. During Lloyd-Jones's lifetime, British churches realized too late the mess they had created. Relying for so long on their ancestors' considerable legacy, many churches could not feel the foundation crumbling beneath them. Despite his myriad pleas, Lloyd-Jones never persuaded the bulk of evangelicals to pursue the God who can do in a moment what incremental organization can hardly accomplish in half a century.

"And content with that, we spend our lives in busy activism, instead of pausing to realize the possibilities, instead of realizing our own failure, and realizing that we are not attracting anyone to Christ, and that they probably see nothing in us that makes them desiring to come to him," Lloyd-Jones said. "The inevitable and constant preliminary to revival has always been a thirst for God, a thirst, a living thirst for a knowledge of the living God, and a longing and a burning desire to see him acting, manifesting himself and his power, rising, and scattering his enemies."[4]

This is where Lloyd-Jones changed my (Collin's) life. For I am too content to pursue my own agenda for reforming the church and reaching the culture. Rarely do I display what Lloyd-Jones called the "terrible seriousness" of Robert Murray McCheyne, a man deeply grieved by a world that does not glorify God by heeding his one and only Son, Jesus Christ.[5] This burden drives serious believers to intercessory prayer for God to save or stifle sinners while reviving his church. I pray for revival, but I rarely invest that prayer with faith that emerges from my surest convictions. This book is for Christians who want to bring their lives in line with their deepest beliefs. This book won't make church committee meetings shorter, can't guarantee greater happiness, and doesn't offer any ready-made revival formula. But by taking you back to days when God tore open the heavens and gave this world a glimpse of blissful eternity, it might stir you to offer prayers that move God.

This book does not attempt to exhaustively recount the history of revivals. Our goal is not mere transmission of historical fact. Of course, we would still heartily encourage motivated readers to chase footnotes and read the full first-person accounts for themselves. We will attempt to show you consistencies between the revivals spread across time and space, but we don't pretend to fully understand when and why God sends revivals. We do, however, recognize the privileged role such accounts have played in the history of revivals. For many years it was common for evangelicals to read stories of revival around the world. Some have been stirred to holy jealousy for God to pour out his Holy Spirit in a fresh, dramatic way on their churches, towns, regions, and nations. This practice reminded believers that we need nothing else, nothing less than the power of God to prevail over the enemies that prey on our complacency. God has given us this means for encouraging us to persevere. As a pioneer in the genre of revival narratives, colonial American pastor Jonathan Edwards recognized his responsibility to share the stories of remarkable events he had witnessed.

"There is no one thing that I know of which God has made such a means of promoting his work amongst us, as the news of others' conversion," Edwards wrote. "This has been owned in awakening sinners, engaging them earnestly to seek the same blessing, and in quickening saints."[6]

Indeed, Edwards went so far as to say that that example contributed to every outpouring of the Holy Spirit in revival.[7] "It has been found by experience that the tidings of remarkable effects of the power and grace of God in any place, tend greatly to awaken and engage the minds of persons in other places."[8] Lloyd-Jones called reading church history "the greatest tonic to a drooping spirit."[9] How many attending and even working in churches today would say the same? We have grown quite familiar with the church's many shortcomings. Standing on our contemporary pedestals, armed with merciless hindsight, we can identify periods when those who claim the name of Christ have fallen so obviously short of his standard. But who can identify those times when the Spirit descended on Connecticut, Wales, New York, Rwanda, India, China, and elsewhere? Who can recall the names of those faithful believers who lived to tell us their remarkable stories? If the church's opponents will use church history against us, we might as well claim our rightful inheritance.

"Fortunately, we have this long record, the history of God's dealings with his people in past ages and centuries, going right away back to the beginning and origin of the human race," Lloyd-Jones said. "And there is nothing, surely, that is of more priceless value to us and to the Church in general than to be familiar with this very history. God does not merely give us teaching, he gives us history."[10]

Some will inevitably wonder whether we can trust these stories. Surely some enthusiastic proponents in the church and even in the media exaggerated for effect. Indeed, they sometimes did. But these events unfolded in broad daylight. Anyone was free to step forward and deny the accounts. Some did, but many of these critics were themselves discredited for misleading audiences according to their own biases. We have done our best to sift through the dross and present you with the most compelling, most reliable stories. May they challenge your assumptions, deepen your love for God and neighbor, and inspire you to petition the God of all grace for revival in our day. We pray with Lloyd-Jones: "Let us lay hold upon Him and plead with Him to vindicate His own truth and the doctrines which are so dear to our hearts, that the church may be revived and masses of people may be saved."[11]

Collin Hansen and John Woodbridge

NOTES

1. D. M. Lloyd-Jones, "Revival: An Historical and Theological Survey," in *The Puritans: Their Origins and Successors; Addresses Delivered at the Puritan and Westminster Conferences 1959–1978* (Carlisle, Pa.: Banner of Truth Trust, 1987), 19.

2. Martyn Lloyd-Jones, *Revival* (Wheaton, Ill.: Crossway, 1987), 35.

3. Lloyd-Jones, "Revival: An Historical and Theological Survey," 18.

4. Lloyd-Jones, *Revival*, 90–91.

5. Ibid., 66.

6. Jonathan Edwards, "A Narrative of Surprising Conversions," in *Jonathan Edwards on Revival* (Carlisle, Pa.: Banner of Truth Trust, 1965), 40.

7. Jonathan Edwards, "The Distinguishing Marks of a Work of the Spirit of God," in *Jonathan Edwards on Revival* (Carlisle, Pa.: Banner of Truth Trust, 1965), 99.

8. Jonathan Edwards, "The Great Awakening," in *The Works of Jonathan Edwards*, ed. C. C. Goen (New Haven, Conn.: Yale University Press, 1972), 529.

9. Lloyd-Jones, *Revival*, 312.

10. Ibid., 281.

11. Lloyd-Jones, "Revival: An Historical and Theological Survey," 23.

CHAPTER 1

BIBLICAL FOUNDATIONS AND THEOLOGY OF REVIVAL

Scottish doctor William Mackay felt drawn to a biblical text that had stirred Christians before him to pray for revival. Like many other favored revival passages, it came from the Old Testament. Reflecting on God's mighty works in redemptive history, the prophet Habakkuk grew emboldened to pray for revival, though judgment and exile loomed for disobedient Judah.

> Lord, I have heard of your fame;
>> I stand in awe of your deeds, O Lord.
> Renew them in our day,
>> in our time make them known;
>> in wrath remember mercy.

Habakkuk 3:2

Mackay wrote the hymn "Revive Us Again" in 1863 and revised it in 1867 shortly before he pursued a call to pastoral ministry. Ira Sankey, the famed musician who accompanied D. L. Moody's evangelistic meetings, included Mackay's tune in his compilation *Gospel Hymns and Sacred Songs*, published in 1875. "Revive Us Again" echoed the heart cry of Christians such as Moody who fondly remembered the great transatlantic awakenings between 1857 and 1859.

> We praise Thee, O God, for the Son of Thy love,
> For Jesus who died and is now gone above.

We praise Thee, O God, for Thy Spirit of light,
Who has shown us our Savior and scattered our night.

All glory and praise to the Lamb that was slain,
Who has borne all our sins and has cleansed every stain.
Revive us again; fill each heart with Thy love;
May each soul be rekindled with fire from above.

Hallelujah, Thine the glory! Hallelujah, amen!
Hallelujah, Thine the glory! Revive us again.[1]

Like many prayers that prevail, Mackay's hymn quotes Scripture back to its divine author. The word for "revive," translated by the New International Version as "renew" in Habakkuk 3:2, comes from the Hebrew word *chaya*, meaning "to bring back to life." The concept of revival, however, extends far beyond occurrences of this word in the Old Testament. Indeed, biblical history includes several occasions when God revived his people by giving them new spiritual life. Before we turn to stories of revival that stretch and stir, we should look to Scripture for which to understand better precedents, patterns, and principles of revival. Jonathan Edwards reminds us that God's Word provides us with the distinguishing marks of an authentic work of the Holy Spirit.

Up from the Depths of Depravity

The Israelites had already suffered several tragic periods of spiritual decline, but the book of Judges ends with an especially devastating thud. "In those days Israel had no king; everyone did as he saw fit" (Judg. 21:25). The problem would not be solved by hereditary monarchy, a point so tragically illustrated by Israel's first king, Saul. The Israelites needed to recognize and acknowledge Yahweh, their one true king. Instead, they persisted in sin. Israel lost the ark of the covenant in battle with the Philistines (1 Sam. 4). Yet no matter what Israel had done, God would not allow this travesty to continue. He demonstrated his exclusive divinity by embarrassing the false Philistine god, Dagon (1 Sam. 5). The Philistines couldn't wait to return the ark to Israel. Still, the ark languished for twenty years before King David finally brought it to Zion (2 Sam. 6).

When the ark returned, Israel experienced the fruit of revival. The entire nation joined their king singing songs of praise to their God. David "danced before the LORD with all his might" (2 Sam. 6:14). During revival, God's people may break out in emotional demonstrations of thanksgiving. They do not intend to attract attention. But they might prompt skepticism from those who do not share their delight in God.[2] When David led the parade into Jerusalem, his wife, Michal, one of Saul's daughters, watched him from a window above. "And when she saw King David leaping and dancing before the LORD, she despised him in her heart" (2 Sam. 6:16). Revival doesn't sweep up everyone, and those standing on the sidelines can become the most outspoken critics. Responding to Michal, David challenged her by displaying his passion for the Lord (2 Sam. 6:21). Revivals may unfortunately spawn extrabiblical experiences that divert attention from God. But spontaneous excitement for the things of God ought not discredit revival.

What was bad under the judges turned worse under the rule of Judah's King Ahaz. He closed the temple (2 Chron. 28:24) and went so far as to burn his own sons as an offering (2 Kings 16:3; 2 Chron. 28:3). The northern tribes of Israel had even teamed up with Syria to besiege Judah's capital, Jerusalem (2 Kings 16:5). To fight them off, Ahaz plundered the temple to buy Assyria's military assistance. As if it weren't bad enough that Israel and Judah warred against one other, Ahaz's strategy was fatally shortsighted. Assyria would seek to divide and conquer them both. But Ahaz would not listen to the warnings delivered by the Lord through Isaiah and other prophets.

The same year Isaiah was called by God to serve as his mouthpiece, Ahaz's wife, Abijah, gave birth to a son, Hezekiah. He survived his murderous father and ascended to the throne of Judah when he was twenty-five years old. Scripture tells us the turnaround was immediate. Hezekiah's devotion to Yahweh inspired a national revival with drastic spiritual and political consequences. The first thing Hezekiah did was throw open the temple doors his father had closed (2 Chron. 29:3). He lit a charge in the priests and Levites, commanding them to consecrate themselves and clean up the temple. They offered sacrifices to Yahweh and orchestrated a grand temple reopening that would have made David proud. Accompanied by instruments from David's time, they sang psalms he wrote (2 Chron. 29:26, 30). Like his forefather David, Hezekiah pursued God with passion. "Hezekiah trusted in the LORD, the God of Israel. There was no one like him among all the kings of Judah, either before him or after him. He held fast to the LORD and did not cease to follow him; he kept the commands the LORD had given Moses" (2 Kings 18:5–6). Still, Hezekiah and the rest of Judah rightly recognized who deserved all the credit. No one but God could have changed their situation so drastically, so quickly (2 Chron. 29:36).

Assyria, though, wasn't impressed with the new spiritual vitality. As they had plundered Israel, they planned to plunder Judah. In Hezekiah's fourteenth year as king, the Assyrians took all of Judah's fortified cities except Jerusalem. Like his father, Hezekiah first tried to buy off the Assyrian king, even plundering the temple once more for silver and gold. But this confrontation wasn't about Hezekiah. The Assyrians taunted Yahweh himself. Standing where Judah's army could hear him, and speaking in their native tongue, an Assyrian official warned, "Do not let Hezekiah persuade you to trust in the LORD when he says, 'The LORD will surely deliver us; this city will not be given into the hand of the king of Assyria'" (2 Kings 18:30).

Hezekiah was scared. Isolated and outnumbered, Judah could not defend Jerusalem against Assyria. The king sought help from the prophet Isaiah. The great prophet assured him that Yahweh would vindicate himself by confusing Assyria's king and striking him down. Hezekiah pleaded with God to do this thing and save his people. "Now, O LORD our God, deliver us from his hand, so that all kingdoms on earth may know that you alone, O LORD, are God" (2 Kings 19:19). Indeed, an angel of the LORD killed 185,000 Assyrians, and the king's own sons killed their father while he worshiped his god back home in Nineveh (2 Kings 19:35–37). Surely this act of divine deliverance illustrated even more clearly the promise of redemption that Judah had celebrated so joyously in the Passover when Hezekiah took the throne (2 Chron. 30).

Spiritual decline and threatening enemies have often spurred believers to pray for God to send revival. He responds favorably not to exalt earthly leaders but to defend and display the glory of his name. In a moment he brings hope to the most hopeless circumstances. But as quickly as revival comes, it can depart. A generation may rise that does not remember what the Lord has done. Hezekiah's son Manasseh reversed his father's reforms and outdid the surrounding nations in evil (2 Chron. 33:9). Even the revived may ultimately forsake the way of blessing. Secure in his wealth, Hezekiah had opened the national treasury to impress envoys from Babylon. They were impressed, all right. Isaiah prophesied to Hezekiah that the Babylonians would someday return and take all this wealth, and even some of his sons. Yet Hezekiah cared only that there would be peace in his time (2 Kings 20:12–21). Revival fires leave behind smoldering embers.

But at least those embers smolder with life. Josiah, when he was just sixteen years old, followed the example of his great-grandfather Hezekiah and repaired the temple. Perhaps Josiah recalled the promise Yahweh delivered to Solomon when he finished building the temple and palace. Throughout the centuries, believers seeking revival have seized on God's promise that "if my people, who are called by my name, will humble themselves and pray and seek my face and turn from their wicked ways, then will I hear from heaven and will forgive their sin and will heal their land" (2 Chron. 7:14). During Josiah's faithful act of repairing the temple, a priest named Hilkiah discovered the Book of the Law (2 Chron. 34:15). Reading God's Word, Josiah came under conviction as he realized how his predecessors had disobeyed (2 Chron. 34:21). He then led the people of Judah in renewing their vows to keep God's covenant (2 Chron. 34:31–32). Their Passover celebration (2 Chron. 35:18) exceeded even the festival enjoyed by Judah under Hezekiah. Following the characteristic pattern of revivals, recovering Scripture brought conviction, followed by repentance, resulting in rejoicing, because the redeemer God doesn't abandon those who seek his face.

Even when God sent Judah into exile at the hand of the Babylonians, he did not forsake the Jews, nor did he forget his covenant promises. When the Persians displaced the Babylonians, they allowed some of the exiles to return to Jerusalem. We might describe some of the events we read about in Ezra and Nehemiah as revival. It started with the priestly scribe Ezra confessing to God how the exiles had sinned by taking foreign wives. "O my God, I am too ashamed and disgraced to lift up my face to you, my God, because our sins are higher than our heads and our guilt has reached to the heavens. From the days of our forefathers until now, our guilt has been great. Because of our sins, we and our kings and our priests have been subjected to the sword and captivity, to pillage and humiliation at the hand of foreign kings, as it is today" (Ezra 9:6–7). By God's grace, the Jews repented. Everyone listened attentively as Ezra read the Law. He and Nehemiah had to tell the crowds to stop crying from conviction and rejoice instead (Neh. 8:9–10). For one week the Jews who returned celebrated the Festival of Booths that they read about in the Scripture.

Then came time for collective confession. When the Jews assembled together, they started by praising God. "Blessed be your glorious name, and may it be exalted above all blessing and praise" (Neh. 9:5). They recalled the wonders God had performed, beginning with creation. "You alone are the LORD. You made the heavens, even the highest heavens, and all their starry host, the earth and all that is on it, the seas and all that is in them. You give life to everything, and the multitudes of heaven worship you" (Neh. 9:6). They recalled his mighty works of redemption. They remembered the call of Abraham, the deliverance at the Red Sea, the Law of Moses handed down at Mount Sinai, God's patient leading through the desert, and how he displaced the Canaanites from the Promised Land (Neh. 9:7–25). Acknowledging God's justice exacted appropriately against his disobedient people, the Jews nevertheless asked him to recognize their distress (Neh. 9:32–37), and they vowed to follow the Law (Neh. 10:28–39).

By now, a revival pattern has come into focus. Following a period of spiritual decline, someone steps forward to acknowledge failure to live according to God's good and gracious law. Others begin to see the problem, and they turn from their wayward path. God may hear their petition and answer their cry with revival. In the revival that broke out under Ezra and Nehemiah, the role of remembrance stands out. When the people remembered the pattern of human disobedience and divine faithfulness, they cast their cares on the Lord as their only hope. He had saved their ancestors from worse plights. Those who have familiarized themselves with redemptive history learn that God sends revival not merely for their sake, but for the glory of his own name (Ps. 79:9). A God who seeks worship naturally grants revival.

> Restore us again, O God our Savior,
> and put away your displeasure toward us.
> Will you be angry with us forever?
> Will you prolong your anger through all generations?
> Will you not revive us again,
> that your people may rejoice in you?
> Show us your unfailing love, O LORD,
> and grant us your salvation.
>
> Psalm 85:4–7

When they recognize that God sends revival so that his name may be praised, believers understand that no need will ever surpass their need for God himself. You can have signs and wonders, but if you don't have God, you don't have revival. God-centered revivals withstand the temptation to treasure the blessings of revival over the one who blesses. And what blessing is greater than God visiting his people by making his Word known and empowering them to live by it? This is what happens when God rends the heavens and comes down (Isa. 64:1), and when Yahweh lives among his people (Zech. 2:10–12).

Times of Refreshing

As the Old gives way to the New Testament, we do not find a single, simple Greek counterpart to the Hebrew word most commonly associated with revival. Nor do we find an equivalent for the English word, which has been derived from the Latin *revivere*, meaning "to live again."[3] But it's more important to identify evidence for the concept rather than the specific word.

It may appear suspicious that no New Testament figure exhorts the church to pray for this type of blessing. Not a problem, said Martyn Lloyd-Jones. You don't pray for God to send revival when you're living in one. "The church always looks like the church in the New Testament when she is in the midst of revival."[4] For many advocates of revival, including Lloyd-Jones, the events of Pentecost are archetypal. They believe that a revived church will display the traits we read about in Acts 2. Because Christians worship a God of history, it's important to understand Pentecost against the Old Testament backdrop. For first-century Jews, Pentecost had become an occasion to remember and celebrate their covenant-making God, who had delivered the Ten Commandments to Moses on Mount Sinai. Like that remarkable day, the Pentecost of Acts 2 featured fire and a storm's roar (Acts 2:2–3; Ex. 19:16–19). The tongues of fire that rested on Jesus' disciples illumined them to fulfill Israel's calling to shine a light for salvation to the nations.

Drawing inspiration from Pentecost, some revival historians offer it as a repeatable paradigm. Lloyd-Jones argued that "every revival is a repetition of Pentecost, and it is the greatest need of the Christian church at this present hour."[5] There is only one sense in which it cannot be repeated, he said. It was the first in a series of revivals.[6] Enthusiastic reporters have unfailingly described their revival as the second-best in that series. Writing the 1741 preface to Jonathan Edwards's "Distinguishing Marks of a Work of the Spirit of God," William Cooper said he didn't think the world had seen such a wonderful "dispensation of grace" as the colonial revival since Pentecost.[7]

Other theologians have pushed back against the interpretation of Pentecost as the model revival. They note that Pentecost was the long-awaited fulfillment of Joel 2 and Jesus' promise to send the Paraclete after he departed (John 16:5–15). Thus, Pentecost marked a unique turning point in salvation history.[8] Luke did not mention Pentecost, then, to show the church what a revival looks like. Edwards himself, in fact, feared that pursuing the same sort of miracles witnessed during the apostolic age would diminish that special period. Not everything from Pentecost could be repeated. "For my part," Edwards said, "I had rather enjoy the sweet influences of the Spirit, showing Christ's spiritual divine beauty, infinite grace, and dying love, drawing forth the holy exercises of faith, divine love, sweet complacence, and humble joy in God, one quarter of an hour, than to have prophetical visions and revelations the whole year."[9]

There is much we can and must learn about revival from Pentecost. It may not be a perfect paradigm, but we can still identify a pattern consistent with the rest of the biblical record. The Holy Spirit equipped Peter to brush aside the critics (Acts 2:14–15) and interpret the movement of God on the basis of Scripture. He mounted a biblical case for Jesus as Christ and Lord. The crowds were convicted of their sin, "cut to the heart" according to Luke (Acts 2:37), and sought salvation. That day alone, about 3,000 were baptized as Spirit-filled believers in Jesus Christ (Acts 2:41). The joyous scene must have rivaled the Passover celebration led by Hezekiah.

Immediately after this account, we read Luke's inspiring description of the early church's everyday life. We see godly leaders teaching the apostolic message and enjoying their privilege as conduits for God's miraculous work (Acts 2:42–43). The body of believers met one another's practical needs (Acts 2:44–45). In a short time, the family of faith had developed a spiritual bond even stronger than genetics. "They met daily," Lloyd-Jones noted from Acts 2:46. "They could not keep away from one another. Of course not, this marvelous thing had happened, this joy of the Lord, and they wanted to thank him together, and to pray together, to ask him to spread it and to extend it to others."[10]

Extend it, God did. Every day the church's numbers grew. Who wouldn't want to join this community so obviously marked by the love of God? Remarkably, the early church enjoyed the favor of "all the people" (Acts 2:47). Though revivals will always have their detractors, they often attract positive attention from outsiders. We have inherited abundant reports from non-Christian media that aid our study of the history of revivals. The world can't help but notice the revived church.[11] Jerusalem took notice when Peter and John healed the crippled beggar at the temple. After all, he ran around the temple courts, jumping and praising God (Acts 3:1–10). Peter once again took the initiative to proclaim the crucified Jesus as the "Holy and Righteous One" and the "author of life" (Acts 3:14–15). Peter then appealed to the crowd. "Repent, then, and turn to God, so that your sins may be wiped out, that times of refreshing may come from the Lord, and that he may send the Christ, who has been appointed for you—even Jesus" (Acts 3:19–20).

The phrase "times of refreshing" might be the favorite proof text for revival. The word for "refreshing," *anapsychsis*, appears only here in the New Testament. Its rarity indicates we should proceed cautiously when trying to build doctrine on the foundation of this one verse. In his analysis of the New Testament terminology, Max Turner finds no definitive evidence for revival as distinct from the usual expectations for the redeemed church. "From Peter's perspective," Turner writes, "the whole future of the church envisaged (not just segments of it) is that of 'times of refreshment,' or of 'release from oppression/affliction,' and this is simply one of several metaphors for what we might otherwise call the 'messianic age.'"[12]

It may be that what we classify as revival, the apostles understood as the church's expected posture toward God, one another, and the world around them. If so, then we might understand revivals as times when Christians remember and embrace their calling by God's grace and the power of the Holy Spirit. During revival, God answers Paul's prayer for the church of Ephesus. "I pray that out of his glorious riches he may strengthen you with power through his Spirit in your inner being, so that Christ may dwell in your hearts through faith. And I pray that you, being rooted and established in love, may have power, together with all the saints, to grasp how wide and long and high and deep is the love of Christ, and to know this love that surpasses knowledge—that you may be filled to the measure of all the fullness of God" (Eph. 3:16–19).

Suddenly, and for an extended period of time, the church truly knows and demonstrates the power of the Holy Spirit (1 Thess. 1:5). Even Turner acknowledges times in Acts when Luke seems to recognize an exceptional intensification of the Spirit's power.[13] When Peter and John returned from their appearance before the Sanhedrin, they reported back to the church how the chief priests and elders warned them not to preach any longer. So they brought these concerns before the Lord in prayer. The room even shook as the Holy Spirit filled them to boldly proclaim the good news about the resurrected Jesus (Acts 4:23 – 31). Linking the story with Pentecost, Luke added a summary statement about how church members cared for one another's financial needs (Acts 4:32 – 37).[14]

So even within the revived church of the New Testament, certain times stand out as especially blessed. Still, it's worth noting that on these special occasions, God works through means he has already revealed in his Word as the church's calling. Sure, a home may shake and lame beggars will jump for joy. But these miracles point toward greater realities. The beggar's healing testified to the God who raised Jesus from the dead. The house shook with the same power of the Spirit that emboldened their preaching. During revival, the church worships, prays, preaches, and evangelizes, only with intensified force. "In the church there is a genuine revival when she rises and shakes herself from the dust and puts on her beautiful garments, which have been laid aside to her great discomfort and reproach," Heman Humphrey observed after the revivals of 1857 to 1859.[15]

Though God is always present with his people, sometimes he is present beyond all doubt, filling believers with the courage to tackle any challenge. During revival, the church militant catches a glimpse of its future as the church triumphant.

Surprising Works and Anxious Benches

Despite these inspiring biblical examples, agreement on a common definition for revival has so far eluded the church. The task of defining revival theologically threatens to derail any contemporary effort to promote revival by recalling historical accounts. Yet modern-day confusion and dismissal demand that we try for the sake of clarity and fidelity.

As in the Old Testament example of Josiah, revivals have often taken the form of reform movements. Several such groups emerged during the Middle Ages and exhibited the marks of revival. In the late twelfth century, Peter Waldo led a church-planting movement in Catholic Europe that advocated public preaching and Bible study. Other forerunners to the Protestant Reformation include the Brethren of the Common Life in Germany and parts of Holland, John Wycliffe and the Lollards in England, and Jan Hus in Bohemia.

The Protestant Reformation fanned the flames of revival across Europe starting in the early sixteenth century. All over Europe, masses encountered biblical teaching for the first time in their own languages and rediscovered a God who justifies sinners who trust him in faith. In their efforts to reform the Church of England, the Puritans saw revived national interest in biblical interpretation and the practice of piety. Exemplary pastors such as Richard Baxter worked across confessional lines to revive interest in true, heartfelt Christianity during the seventeenth century. The enthusiastic, widespread response to Baxter's work at Kidderminster resembled revival. Meanwhile, Scottish Presbyterians celebrated days-long communion festivals where Christians recovered the exuberance and communal spirit of Pentecost. Presbyterian evangelists traveling through colonial America likewise linked communion with revival.[16]

Other theological streams poured into colonial America from the British Isles during the mid-eighteenth century to feed what would become known as the First Great Awakening. During his journey to America, John Wesley found his faith wanting compared to Moravian believers who weathered a violent storm with calm dispositions. Back home in London, Wesley experienced a dramatic conversion during a Moravian meeting on Aldersgate Street in 1738. Shortly thereafter, he visited the Moravian community in Herrnhut, which had experienced revival in 1727. Due in part to this type of theological cross-pollination, believers in America and the British Isles adopted several continental revival practices from the Moravians, Huguenots, and Salzbergers. These included field preaching, devotional treatises, and camp meetings. America in particular became a remarkable laboratory where several different revival traditions merged to bolster the burgeoning evangelical movement.

Many historians regard Jonathan Edwards as the greatest revival theologian, but he inherited a religious tradition concerned with seeking new outpourings of God's Spirit. According to the *Oxford English Dictionary*, New England Puritan pastor Cotton Mather first gave the term *revival* a technical religious definition.[17] Edwards's grandfather Solomon Stoddard presided over several local revivals during his tenure as pastor in Northampton. Edwards had been primed with an unmatched revival pedigree. Edwards described the sudden and spontaneous outburst of religious fervor in Northampton in 1741 as a "surprising work of God." To be clear, Edwards believed that God employs certain means, such as preaching the Word of God, in order to spur revival. But he did not teach that any series of events could guarantee an outpouring of the Holy Spirit. Only God himself could bestow such a blessing on his people in his own sovereign timing. God apparently favored Northampton, because another revival had previously come upon the people there in 1734–35. "This seems to have been a very *extraordinary* dispensation of providence; God has in many respects gone out of, and much beyond, his usual and *ordinary way*," Edwards wrote in his "Narrative of Surprising Conversions." "The work in this town, and others about us, has been extraordinary on account of the universality of it, affecting all sorts, sober and vicious, high and low, rich and poor, wise and unwise."[18]

Edwards rarely saw dramatic spiritual change in everyday life except from the young. But during revival, even older church members professed newfound vitality. His sermons marshaled the same old arguments, but they suddenly gained traction, and people understood what had previously escaped them. It seemed like almost overnight the town changed unmistakably. Overcome either by distress from sin or by the greatness of God, people talked of nothing but revival. Those yet untouched by the awakening pleaded for God to revive them. Every day felt like Sunday, and everyone seemed to look forward to the Sunday meeting.

"Our public assemblies were then beautiful: the congregation was *alive* in God's service, every one earnestly intent on the public worship, every *hearer* eager to drink in the words of the *minister* as they came from his mouth; the assembly in general were, from time to time, *in tears* while the Word was preached: *some* weeping with sorrow and distress, *others* with joy and love, *others* with pity and concern for the souls of their neighbours," Edwards observed in his narrative.[19]

So how does revival come? Edwards believed nothing could guarantee revival. But he greatly admired the Scottish Concert of Prayer and advocated for this example of unified petitions in his aptly named book *An Humble Attempt to Promote an Explicit Agreement and Visible Union of God's People thro' the World, in Extraordinary Prayer, for the Revival of Religion, and the Advancement of Christ's Kingdom on Earth, Pursuant to Scripture Promise and Prophecies Concerning the Last Time.* He hoped that Christians would pray regularly for revival on Saturday nights, Sunday mornings, and four times each year during days set aside for that sole purpose.[20]

But Edwards contributed perhaps his greatest service to the cause of revival in his writing about discernment. He warned against the anticlerical enthusiasm of the revival's radicals. And he cautioned against making too much out of personal impulses and impressions about the will of God that could not be verified by Scripture. But to the notorious Boston minister and revival critic Charles Chauncy, Edwards himself was the problem. "He mistakes the workings of his own passions for divine communications and fancies himself immediately inspired by the SPIRIT of GOD, when all the while, he is under no other influence than that of an over-heated imagination."[21]

Still, if you carved a Mount Rushmore of American revival, Edwards would be your first choice. Next you would likely turn to Charles Finney. But the differences between the two men illustrate the difficulties of defining revival. Born in 1792, thirty-four years after Edwards died, Finney became the most prominent American revivalist in the nineteenth century. Reacting in part to the Edwardian tradition, Finney taught that only our reluctance hinders revival. "You see why you have not a revival," he said. "It is only because you do not want one."[22] Lecturing from Habakkuk 3:2, Finney explained that religion is a human work. "It is something for man to do," he said. "It consists in obeying God. It is man's duty."[23] On the other hand, Finney believed that no one obeys divine commands unless God intervenes in response to prayer. Yet on the whole, Finney's emphasis on human responsibility contributed to the modern understanding of revivals as events orchestrated in order to elicit a favorable response to evangelistic appeals.

For too long, Finney believed, Christians have waited for God to move, when all along God has gifted the church with everything it needs to spark revival. Finney deployed his theology to identify "new measures" that would yield the fruit of revival, much like wise agricultural practices yield an abundant harvest. The most famous of these measures, the "anxious seat," became a staple of

American evangelism, leading to practices such as the altar call. Finney invited his listeners to come forward and sit in a designated area where he could address them directly or someone could talk with them individually. Claiming that the Bible does not prefer certain measures before others, Finney defended this tactic by appealing to "laws of mind."

"When a person is seriously troubled in mind, everybody knows there is a powerful tendency to conceal it," Finney said. "When a person is borne down with a

Charles Finney expected his "new measures" would result in revival. (Used by permission of Oberlin College Archives.)

sense of his condition, if you can get him willing to have it known, if you can get him to break away from the chains of pride, you have gained an important point towards his conversion."[24]

Finney has not wanted for critics. Some have observed how naturally his theology and new measures aligned with the fledgling American democracy's populist spirit. Others say his theology of conversion leads to manipulation.[25] And several revivals subsequent to Finney, including those covered in this book, did not follow his formula. Even so, Finney's view dominated the revival discussion for decades. Pushing back, Martyn Lloyd-Jones delivered a series of lectures on revival during the one hundredth anniversary of the transatlantic revivals of 1859. According to J. I. Packer, "No concern was nearer to his heart, nor to mine."[26] Over the course of twenty-six Sunday morning services at Westminster Chapel in London, Lloyd-Jones took up Edwards's position and claimed a lengthy historical precedent stretching back to the New Testament. He offered several definitions for revival. Perhaps none surpasses his definition that incorporates all three persons of the Trinity. During revival, Lloyd-Jones taught, the Holy Spirit fills the church with a glimpse of God's glory in the face of Jesus Christ. The church sees in the Cross and Resurrection the occasions when God's justice and love converge. So do his righteousness and mercy, his wrath and incomparable compassion.[27] During revival, the church desires nothing more than to reflect on these glorious truths.[28]

Noting the Old Testament examples, Lloyd-Jones taught that revival begins by awakening sluggish believers. Mere intellectual knowledge comes alive in praise and practice. Some Christians question whether they can claim the name of Christ as they begin to understand their deep sinfulness. But this act of humility is a strong sign that God's grace abounds to them. Awareness of their own sin makes Christians experiencing revival more aware of how their neighbors profane God's name.

So they pray for these neighbors, tell them about God's redemptive work in Christ, and invite them to see Christians gather to worship and hear God's Word. Preachers experience new power to explain Scripture for unbelievers, some of whom come to profess faith in Christ. So while revival begins with the church, its effects do not stop there. Revivals seize the world's attention. Indeed, revival is a corporate event. It may begin with someone specially consecrated to God, but it will spread like wildfire. As with biblical Israel, entire nations may eventually sense the Spirit's presence and power, feeling the conviction of sin and the joy of redemption.

"Revival is a social, corporate thing, touching and transforming communities, large and small. Bible prayers for revival implore God to quicken not *me* but *us*," Packer writes. "God revives his church, and then the new life overflows from the church for the conversion of outsiders and the renovation of society."[29]

Though God alone can instigate revival, the church need not wait idly. God may choose unexpected ways and times to bless our efforts to preach and teach his Word. We can confess our sins known and unknown and forsake them. Above all else, we can pray. When Christians petition God for revival, they acknowledge that all their efforts to organize and contextualize go for naught unless God goes before them. Revival is neither a well-organized evangelistic campaign nor a finely crafted apologetic treatise, though the church may profitably employ such methods. Revival transcends all ordinary ways we comprehend and communicate the grace of Jesus Christ. For reasons known only to him, God occasionally condescends to answer his people's faithful prayers with a special sense of his power and presence. "And that is revival," Lloyd-Jones wrote, "the descent, the outpouring of the Spirit over and above his usual, ordinary work; this amazing, unusual, extraordinary thing, which God in his sovereignty and infinite grace has done to the Church from time to time during the long centuries of her history."[30]

Indeed, neither the biblical record nor Christian history is complete without these stories of revival. When all hope seemed lost, God moved. The world never escapes the reach of his sovereign care. As Heman Humphrey once wrote, the history of the church is "sometimes sparkling in the sunlight; sometimes all but swallowed up in the sands of the desert; breaking out again in the promised land; at one period a wide river, then a contracted rivulet almost hidden for long reaches, and widening again to keep the promise alive, when it seemed to have disappeared for ever in the stagnant marshes of Babylon."[31]

NOTES

1. Kenneth W. Osbeck, *Amazing Grace: 366 Inspiring Hymn Stories for Daily Devotions* (Grand Rapids: Kregel, 1990), 306.

2. Raymond C. Ortlund, Jr., *When God Comes to Church: A Biblical Model for Revival Today* (Grand Rapids: Baker, 2000), 94.

3. Earle E. Cairns, *An Endless Line of Splendor: Revivals and Their Leaders from the Great Awakening to the Present* (Wheaton, Ill.: Tyndale, 1986), 20.

4. D. M. Lloyd-Jones, "Revival: An Historical and Theological Survey," in *The Puritans: Their Origins and Successors; Addresses Delivered at the Puritan and Westminster Conferences 1959–1978* (Carlisle, Pa.: Banner of Truth Trust, 1987), 12.

5. D. Martyn Lloyd-Jones, *The Baptism and Gifts of the Spirit*, ed. Christopher Catherwood (Grand Rapids: Baker, 1984), 441–42.

6. Martyn Lloyd-Jones, *Revival* (Wheaton, Ill.: Crossway, 1987), 199.

7. William Cooper, preface to "The Distinguishing Marks of a Work of the Spirit of God," in *Jonathan Edwards on Revival* (Carlisle, Pa.: Banner of Truth Trust, 1965), 77.

8. Graham A. Cole, *He Who Gives Life: The Doctrine of the Holy Spirit* (Wheaton, Ill.: Crossway, 2007), 233.

9. Jonathan Edwards, "A Narrative of Surprising Conversions," in *Jonathan Edwards on Revival* (Carlisle, Pa.: Banner of Truth Trust, 1965), 141.

10. Lloyd-Jones, *Revival*, 207.

11. Ortlund, *When God Comes to Church*, 133.

12. Max Turner, "Revival in the New Testament?" in *On Revival: A Critical Examination*, eds. Andrew Walker and Kristin Aune (Waynesboro, Ga.: Paternoster, 2003), 8.

13. Ibid., 18.

14. Richard F. Lovelace, *Dynamics of Spiritual Life: An Evangelical Theology of Renewal* (Downers Grove, Ill.: InterVarsity, 1979), 49.

15. Heman Humphrey, *Revival Sketches and Manual* (New York: American Tract Society, 1859), 13.

16. Leigh Eric Schmidt, *Holy Fairs: Scotland and the Making of American Revivalism*, 2nd ed. (Grand Rapids: Eerdmans, 2001), 54.

17. W. R. Ward, *The Protestant Evangelical Awakening* (Cambridge: Cambridge University Press, 1999), 282–83.

18. Edwards, "A Narrative of Surprising Conversions," 19.

19. Ibid., 14.

20. George Marsden, *Jonathan Edwards: A Life* (New Haven, Conn.: Yale, 2003), 334–35.

21. Charles Chauncy, *Enthusiasm Described and Caution'd Against* (Boston: S. Eliot Cornhill & Blanchard, 1742), 3.

22. Charles G. Finney, "When a Revival Is to Be Expected," in *Lectures on Revivals of Religion* (New York: Leavitt, Lord & Co., 1835), 32.

23. Charles G. Finney, "What a Revival of Religion Is," in *Lectures on Revivals of Religion* (New York: Leavitt, Lord & Co., 1835), 9.

24. Charles G. Finney, "Measure to Promote Revivals," in *Lectures on Revivals of Religion* (New York: Leavitt, Lord & Co., 1835), 247.

25. Lovelace, *Dynamics of Spiritual Life*, 252.

26. Lloyd-Jones, *Revival*, v.

27. Ibid., 248–49.

28. Iain Murry, a colleague of Lloyd-Jones's at Westminster Chapel, has carefully defined revival by examining Scripture. He contends that "revival is an outpouring of the Holy Spirit, brought about by the intercession of Christ, resulting in a new degree of life in the churches and a widespread movement of grace among the unconverted. It is an extraordinary communication of the Spirit of God, a superabundance of the Spirit's operations, and enlargement of his manifest power." Iain H. Murray, *Pentecost — Today? The Biblical Basis for Understanding Revival* (Carlisle, Pa.: Banner of Truth Trust, 1998), 23–24.

29. J. I. Packer, *Keep in Step with the Spirit* (Tarrytown, N.Y.: Revel, 1984), 256.

30. Lloyd-Jones, *Revival*, 54.

31. Humphrey, *Revival Sketches and Manual*, 11.

CHAPTER 2

"SURPRISING" SIGNS OF THE NEW BIRTH

First Great Awakening, 1730s to 1740s
NORTH AMERICA

While colonial America may seem to be a model of religious virtue, Christianity rode the ups and downs of life on an exciting, dangerous frontier. Following the devastating King Philip's War in 1676, in which half of the English settlements in Massachusetts and Connecticut were destroyed, pastors urged Christians to renew their commitments to God and one another. Nevertheless, rock-ribbed New England, home to the descendants of Puritans who risked everything to settle in a strange new world, suffered from an identity crisis. The emotional exhortations of past Puritan preaching had given way in many quarters to rational lectures that prized reason over affections, the mind over the heart.

Still, small pockets of piety stood out. Under the leadership of Solomon Stoddard, the congregation at Northampton in western Massachusetts experienced five fleeting revivals between 1679 and 1718. A bigger revival touched Connecticut between 1720 and 1722. Hundreds of new Christians joined churches. Then in 1727, a shocking earthquake shook up Northampton and the rest of New England. Always searching for evidence of God's plan, New England's leading pastors warned their congregations to repent, because God might shake the earth once more with a special movement of the Holy Spirit.

This emphasis on "seasons of revival" marked a "new elaboration" of the Protestant Reformation, according to historian Thomas Kidd.[1] During what would come to be known as the First Great Awakening, a diverse group of Protestant movements, ranging from Continental Pietism, Scots-Irish Presbyterianism, and Anglo-American Puritanism, would cooperate and swap ideas on how to promote and sustain revivals. Several leaders would emerge and leave behind a lasting legacy. But few shaped American religion like Stoddard's grandson, Jonathan Edwards.

Jonathan Edwards

Born in 1703, Edwards attended Yale and succeeded his grandfather, who died in 1729, as senior pastor of the Congregational church in Northampton. Edwards lost this pastorate in 1750, but not before God visited Northampton with two major revivals. Shortly before he died in 1758, Edwards became the president of the College of New Jersey, later renamed Princeton University, a school founded in 1746 to train ministers who supported the Great Awakening.

"[Edwards] was the first to publicize revivals, he became their principal theorist, and he was long revered as the greatest theologian of revivalism, the nation's most influential theological tradition," biographer George Marsden writes.[2]

Edwards inherited the expectation of revival from his grandfather and fellow Puritan ministers. We remember Edwards as a deathly serious preacher, and he certainly

Jonathan Edwards stoked anticipation for revival by writing "A Faithful Narrative of the Surprising Work of God" about the Northampton awakening. (Portrait of Jonathan Edwards by Joseph Badger, courtesy of Yale University Art Gallery, bequest of Eugene P. Edwards, 1937.)

rubbed some church members the wrong way. But he longed to see everyone find ultimate, eternal joy in the Creator and Savior. So when he worried over the young people in his community, he didn't just want them to live morally upright lives. He was concerned for their souls as well. Their sins revealed a spiritual longing only God could meet.

Scarcity of land and livelihood led to social upheaval in Northampton during the 1730s. On average, men waited until they were twenty-nine to marry. Women waited until they were twenty-five. As a result, an alarming number of children were born out of wedlock. Then in June 1734, a widely admired young man died unexpectedly. Edwards preached from Psalm 90:5–6: "You sweep men away in the sleep of death; they are like the new grass of the morning—though in the morning it springs up new, by evening it is dry and withered." The untimely death and Edwards's weighty sermon left an impression. Edwards reported that the young people became serious and began studying the Bible and praying together in small groups.

Edwards spurred on the revival with one his most famous sermons, preached in August 1734. In "A Divine and Supernatural Light," Edwards contended, "There is a difference between having a rational judgment that honey is sweet, and having a sense of its sweetness. A man may have the former, that knows not how honey tastes; but a man can't have the latter, unless he has an idea of the taste of honey in his mind."[3] With this analogy, Edwards sought to show the difference between merely having knowledge about God and experiencing his love and the truth of his Word. Yet Edwards still gave careful attention to knowledge. He preached a two-sermon series in November, emphasizing that only those who trust in Christ, not human virtue or goodness, are justified before God.

The revival continued through December, when one of the town's most promiscuous young women converted and reached out to her rowdy friends. In his exuberance over the Northampton awakening, Edwards wrote "A Faithful Narrative of the Surprising Work of God," the first such detailed account of revival. He explained several ways the community had changed. Everyone seemed more focused on eternity. Many new converts professed faith in Christ. The town exhibited better morals. And church members showed higher regard for Scripture and kept the Sabbath. Some thirty-two other towns were eventually visited with the revival that first broke out in Northampton. Edwards's narrative circulated back in the Old World and created a longing for revival among British evangelicals, including the famed Methodist preacher John Wesley, who read the report in 1738 shortly after his Aldersgate conversion.

Yet by the time the outside world learned about the Northampton revival, it had come to an abrupt and tragic end. Only two days after he finished writing his narrative, Edwards's uncle Joseph Hawley, a revered town leader, slit his own throat and died. Before committing suicide on June 1, 1735, Hawley had fallen into depression as he feared spending eternity in hell. Later, several other esteemed church members reported hearing voices telling them to slit their throats. It appeared to Edwards that the God-honoring revival had incurred the wrath of Satan, who sought to quell the joyous outburst.

Indeed, Edwards conveyed a terrifyingly vivid sense of Satan's schemes and the reality of hell, especially in his later preaching. During a visit to Enfield, Connecticut, on July 8, 1741, he preached his most famous sermon, "Sinners in the Hands of an Angry God." Due to screaming and other emotional displays from the congregation, Edwards could not even finish the sermon with an appeal to accept God's grace. The people of Enfield were too terrified by his vivid description of God's judgment and hell:

"The God that holds you over the pit of hell, much as one holds a spider, or some loathsome insect over the fire, abhors you, and is dreadfully provoked: his wrath towards you burns like fire; he looks upon you as worthy of nothing else, but to be cast into the fire; he is of purer eyes than to bear to have you in his sight; you are ten thousand times more abominable in his eyes, than the most hateful venomous serpent is in ours."[4]

More than anything else, this sermon has shaped popular understanding of Edwards and the revival, which began to intensify in 1740. As a result, many observers dismiss the awakening as a vestige of a happily bygone past. Yet Edwards believed that he loved people by warning them of hell. Eternity separated from God is so terrible, Edwards believed, that a minister who explains it dispassionately contradicts himself.

"If I am in danger of going to hell, I should be glad to know as much as possibly I can of the dreadfulness of it," he said. "If I am very prone to neglect due care to avoid it, he does me the best kindness who does most to represent to me the truth of the case, that sets forth my misery and danger in the liveliest manner."[5]

The Moravian Pietists

Even as the Northampton revival faded in 1735, other colonies were caught up in the early stages of what came to be known as the First Great Awakening. During a visit to New York, Edwards heard about revivals in New Jersey led by Gilbert Tennent and Theodorus Jacobus Frelinghuysen. Born in Germany, Frelinghuysen arrived in New York in 1720 and almost immediately stirred things up. An ordained Dutch Reformed minister, he warned against pastors who did not give sufficient evidence of a true, life-altering conversion. Frelinghuysen was a Pietist, an adherent of the Protestant renewal movement based in continental Europe that encouraged heartfelt religion with practices such as small-group meetings. Frelinghuysen linked causes with Tennent, an Ulster Scottish Presbyterian, when he became pastor of a church in Frelinghuysen's parish. Frelinghuysen taught Tennent how to preach the new birth, an emphasis drawn from Jesus' teaching in John 3:3. "I tell you the truth, no one can see the kingdom of God unless he is born again."

Like the Puritans, Pietists lamented that the full promise of the Reformation had not yet been truly realized. So they sought to put their faith to work. German Pietist August Francke, who converted in 1687 and later became a theology professor, built an evangelical outpost in Halle that cared for orphans, organized foreign missions, and printed Christian literature, including accounts of revival. Venerable Boston minister Cotton Mather considered Halle

John Wesley's heart was "strangely warmed" during a Moravian meeting. (Courtesy of the Museum of the Billy Graham Center, Wheaton, Illinois.)

a hopeful sign that God was working to revive his people. Another German Pietist community, founded by Nikolaus von Zinzendorf and named Herrnhut, similarly stirred the colonial longing for revival. So-called Moravians traveled around the world, including the colonies, as missionaries. Their most famous convert was John Wesley. The world would never be the same as Wesley and his brother Charles went on to lead a renewal movement that pursued evangelism and holiness with biblical zeal.

George Whitefield

The Moravians left a lasting impression on another young preacher, George Whitefield. Before he turned twenty-three, Whitefield was a household name in London, where he preached more than a hundred times in five months at the end of 1737. Then at the urging of John and Charles Wesley, friends from his Oxford days, Whitefield headed for the fledgling colony of Georgia. But he encountered hostility in Savannah because the Wesleys had hastily left behind the mission there in disrepair. Whitefield planned to improve the conditions by starting an orphanage, modeled on the Pietist outpost in Halle. Whitefield raised money for the orphanage but stayed only three months in Georgia before heading home to England. That's when his life and preaching as we know it changed forever. Back on the other side of the Atlantic, Whitefield explored the potential for a new preaching style being practiced elsewhere on the isles. Blocked from church pulpits by hostile pastors, Whitefield experimented with open-air preaching in February 1739. Only one

George Whitefield preached the gospel message about new birth in Christ to the masses.
(Courtesy of the Billy Graham Center, Wheaton, Illinois.)

week later, 10,000 turned out to hear him. Three months later, as many as 60,000 turned out to hear him preach in London.

Gifted with a sonorous voice and curiously cross-eyed, Whitefield appealed for listeners to experience the new birth. It wasn't enough for them to sign an orthodox creed or live morally. They must be born again.

> The sum of the matter is this: Christianity includes morality, as grace does reason; but if we are only mere *moralists*, if we are not *inwardly* wrought upon, and changed by the powerful operations of the *Holy Spirit*, and our moral actions proceed from a principle of a *New Nature*, however we may call ourselves Christians, it is to be feared we shall be found naked at the Great Day, and in the number of those, who vainly depend on their own righteousness, and not on the righteousness of Jesus Christ, imputed to and inherent in them, as necessary to their eternal salvation.... It is not enough to turn from *profaneness* to *civility*; but thou must turn from *civility* to *godliness*. Not only *some*, but *all things* must become *new* in thy soul. It will

profit thee but little to do many things, if yet some *one thing* thou lackest. In short, thou must not be only an *almost*, but *altogether* a *New Creature*, or in vain thou hopest for a saving interest *in* Christ.[6]

New England pastors were well aware of the excitement that attended Whitefield's appeal. Writing from Boston, Thomas Prince captured some of their enthusiasm: "We were yet more surpriz'd to hear of his Preaching the *Doctrines* of the *Martyrs* and other *Reformers*, which were the same our *Fore-Fathers* brought over hither: Particularly the great Doctrines of *Original Sin*, of *Regeneration by the* DIVINE SPIRIT, *Justification by Faith only*, etc. and this with amazing Assiduity Power and Success: which extraordinary Appearance, especially in the *Church of England*, together with the vast Multitudes of People that flock'd to hear him, drew our Attention to every Thing that was published concerning him."[7]

Revival Assessed and Defended

Benjamin Franklin, who was working as a publisher at the time, became a prominent defender and friend of Whitefield despite rejecting the evangelist's message. Franklin met Whitefield during his tour through Philadelphia in 1739, which followed a stint in Ireland. As in London, local ministers chafed at Whitefield and denied his requests to preach from their pulpits. So once again he took his message about the new birth directly to the masses. Franklin was impressed by the huge, diverse crowds who turned out to hear Whitefield. He was even more impressed that they actually liked what he had to say, "notwithstanding his common abuse of them, by assuring them that they were naturally half beasts and half devils." But Franklin couldn't deny the evidence of revival that accompanied Whitefield's visit. "It was wonderful to see the change soon made in the manners of our inhabitants. From being thoughtless or indifferent about religion, it seem'd as if all the world were growing religious, so that one could not walk thro' the town in an evening without hearing psalms sung in different families of every street."[8]

While they did not always see eye to eye, Whitefield and Franklin shared a genuine friendship until the evangelist died in 1770. When critics accused Whitefield of deception and dishonesty, Franklin often came to the defense of the man whose sermons and journals he published. He even put some of his vaunted scientific acumen to use in calculating that more than 30,000 people could hear Whitefield preaching at one time.

"He had a loud and clear voice, and articulated his words and sentences so perfectly, that he might be heard and understood at a great distance, especially as his auditories, however numerous, observ'd the most exact silence.... Both streets were fill'd with his hearers to a considerable distance."[9]

Whitefield's biggest colonial crowds awaited him in Boston, where he arrived on September 18, 1740. Unlike those in Philadelphia, many of Boston's pastors were willing to host Whitefield. Three days later he addressed some 15,000 on Boston Common, an impressive number for one of the largest colonial cities. His farewell sermon in Boston, population 17,000, attracted an even larger crowd of 20,000 on October 12.

Surely preaching before these throngs excited Whitefield. But he also looked forward to a face-to-face meeting with Edwards. Whitefield had written Jonathan Edwards in November 1739 to see if he could visit the scene of the famous revival from 1734 and 1735. Edwards responded but sought to dampen expectations, knowing Northampton no longer enjoyed revival. Nevertheless, Whitefield arrived in Northampton in October 1740. He stayed with the Edwards family, who were accustomed to hosting visitors who wanted to learn from Jonathan. Both men were deeply affected by the meeting. Edwards cautioned the younger minister not to be so hasty in judging fellow pastors as unconverted. Once Whitefield moved on, he even warned his own congregation not to be deceived by fleeting religious enthusiasm. After all, many who had been suddenly smitten with Whitefield earlier had lost their affections for Christ when the previous revival ended.

Nevertheless, Whitefield's visit altered the course of Edwards's ministry and family life. Despite their differing styles and personalities, Edwards became one of Whitefield's leading public advocates. Edwards had invited Whitefield to discuss spiritual matters with four of his daughters, after which Jonathan identified a change in their lives. For his part, Whitefield, still unmarried, enjoyed spending time with the large family. Sarah in particular impressed him. "Mrs. Edwards is adorned with a meek and quiet spirit; she talked solidly of the things of God, and seemed to be such a helpmeet for her husband." Later he prayed that God "would be pleased to send me a daughter of Abraham to be my wife."[10] Sarah, Edwards's wife, was impressed with Whitefield too as she listened to his sermons in Northampton.

"He makes less of doctrines than our American preachers generally do, and aims more at affecting the heart," she wrote to her brother. "He is a born orator. You have already heard of his deep-toned, yet clear and melodious voice. It is perfect music. It is wonderful to see what a spell he casts over an audience by proclaiming the simplest truths of the Bible. I have seen upwards of a thousand people hang on his words with breathless silence, broken only by an occasional half-suppressed sob."[11]

Though Whitefield cultivated friendships with wealthy printers and famous pastors, his role in spreading the revival depended on support from the masses. Nothing illustrates this appeal so vividly as the account of Nathan Cole, a farmer who was thirty years old when Whitefield visited Middletown, Connecticut, on October 23, 1740, less than a week after Whitefield left the Edwards family in Northampton. Cole expected his works would save him. But he couldn't resist the opportunity to hear from the renowned evangelist for himself. Even as a farmer, Cole was acquainted with the details of Whitefield's evangelistic tours and the accompanying revival.

> Then on a Sudden, in the morning about 8 or 9 of the Clock there came a messenger and said Mr Whitfield preached at Hartford and Weathersfield yesterday and is to preach at Middletown this morning at ten of the Clock, I was in my field at Work, I dropt my tool that I had in my hand and ran home to

my wife telling her to make ready quickly to go and hear Mr Whitfield preach at Middletown, then run to my pasture for my horse with all my might; fearing that I should be too late; having my horse I with my wife soon mounted the horse and went forward as fast as I thought the horse could bear ...; all the while fearing we should be too late to hear the Sermon, for we had twelve miles to ride double in little more than an hour and we went round by the upper housen parish.

And when we came within about half a mile or a mile of the Road that comes down from Hartford Weathersfield and Stepney to Middletown; on high land I saw before me a Cloud or fogg rising; I first thought it came from the great River, but as I came nearer the Road, I heard a noise something like a low rumbling thunder and presently found it was the noise of Horses feet coming down the Road and this Cloud was a Cloud of dust made by the Horses feet; ... every horse seemed to go with all his might to carry his rider to hear news from heaven for the saving of Souls....

We went down in the Stream but heard no man speak a word all the way for 3 miles but every one pressing forward in great haste and when we got to Middletown old meeting house there was a great Multitude it was said to be 3 or 4000 of people Assembled together; we dismounted and shook of[f] our Dust; and the ministers were then Coming to the meeting house; I turned and looked towards the Great River and saw the ferry boats Running swift backward and forward bringing over loads of people and the Oars Rowed nimble and quick; every thing men horses and boats seemed to be Struggling for life; The land and banks over the river looked black with people and horses all along the 12 miles I saw no man at work in his field, but all seemed to be gone.

When I saw Mr Whitfield come upon the Scaffold he Lookt almost angelical; a young, Slim, slender, youth before some thousands of people with a bold undaunted Countenance, and my hearing how God was with him every where as he came along it Solemnized my mind; and put me into a trembling fear before he began to preach; for he looked as if he was Cloathed with authority from the Great God; and a sweet sollome solemnity sat upon his brow And my hearing him preach, gave me a heart wound; By Gods blessing: my old Foundation was broken up, and I saw that my righteousness would not save me; then I was convinced of the doctrine of Election: and went right to quarrelling with God about it; because that all I could do would not save me; and he had decreed from Eternity who should be saved and who not.[12]

The Controversy over "Religious Affections"

When he finished his New England tour, Whitefield asked his friend Gilbert Tennent to follow in his wake and build upon his work. Tennent, a Presbyterian from New Jersey, had ignited controversy with his 1740 sermon "The Danger of an Unconverted Ministry." In a society where ministers had been afforded deference, Tennent's sermon signified great battles over the revival that would come. "As a faithful Ministry is a great Ornament, Blessing, and Comfort, to the Church of GOD; even the Feet of such Messengers are beautiful," Tennent said. "So on the contrary, an ungodly Ministry is a great Curse and Judgment: These Caterpillars labour to devour every green Thing."[13]

Yet when Tennent visited Yale College in 1741, the revival spread. One student, Samuel Hopkins, testified to the power of Tennent's preaching. Thousands came under conviction that God hated their sins and would consign them to hell if they did not repent. Even some Yale professors confessed that they had not been born again until now. Later, when the revival grew more divisive, Yale's rector and tutors would publish a letter against the most visible revival preacher, Whitefield. But for now, revival prevailed. Hopkins identified several students whose zeal stood out. He approached one of these students, David Brainerd, and admitted that he had no "religious affections." Brainerd explained that he needed to be born again. Hopkins retreated to his prayer closet, where he sensed God's presence in a new way.[14] As a sign of the revival's revolutionary effects, Brainerd was expelled during his junior year when he said a tutor had "no more grace than a chair."

As the revival grew, so did the number of detractors. Not all who supported the revival condoned Tennent's judgments against ministers. Surely few of these moderate ministers sanctioned the increasingly wild antics of James Davenport, another Yale graduate. Radicals such as Davenport emphasized personal, immediate assurance by the Holy Spirit. They claimed the ability to discern whether the Spirit dwelled in others and named those who allegedly did not have the Spirit. They did not believe ministers needed education, so they were hardly swayed by educated ministers who criticized them. They welcomed unusual demonstrations of the Spirit from members of the lower strata of society.

The radicals put Edwards and his allies in a bind. Edwards was hesitant to regard emotional displays as dangerous. In *Some Thoughts Concerning the Present Revival of Religion*, published in 1742, he described a woman who fainted as she sensed the fullness of Christ's love and power. Her soul was lost in God, according to Edwards. He did not explain that he was talking about his wife, Sarah. She recalled:

That night, which was Thursday night, Jan. 28, was the sweetest night I ever had in my life. I never before, for so long a time together, enjoyed so much of the light, and rest, and sweetness of heaven in my soul, but without the least agitation of body during the whole time. The great part of the night I lay awake, sometimes asleep, and sometimes between sleeping and waking. But all night I continued in a constant, clear, and lively sense of the heavenly sweetness of Christ's excellent and transcendent love, of his nearness to me, and of my dearness to him; with an inexpressibly sweet calmness of soul in an entire rest in him. I seemed to myself to perceive a glow of divine love come down from the heart of Christ in heaven, into my heart, in a constant stream, like a stream or pencil of sweet light. At the same time, my heart and soul all flowed out in love to Christ; so that there seemed to be a constant flowing and reflowing of heavenly and divine love, from Christ's heart to mine; and I appeared to myself to float or swim, in these bright, sweet beams of the love of Christ, like the motes swimming in the beams of the sun, or the streams of his light which come in at the window.[15]

Such accounts did not impress Charles Chauncy, pastor of Boston's First Church. While Jonathan Edwards defended the revival by preaching in Northampton about the distinguishing marks of a work of the Spirit of God, Chauncy spoke that same day about *An Unbridled Tongue a Sure Evidence, that our Religion is Hypocritical and Vain*. Chauncy, who would later teach universalism, condemned Edwards and other revival leaders for judging their neighbors as unregenerate. To defend the revival against critiques from Chauncy and his allies, Boston pastor Thomas Prince Sr. convened a convention of moderate pastors on July 7, 1743. They produced a statement that reaffirmed their belief that God was at work but also urged revived Christians to deal charitably with skeptics.

Indeed it is not to be denied that in some Places many Irregularities and Extravagancies have been permitted to accompany it, which we would deeply lament and bewail before GOD, and look upon our selves oblig'd, for the Honour of the HOLY SPIRIT, and of his blessed Operations on the Souls of Men, to bear a publick and faithful Testimony against; tho' at the same Time it is to be acknowledg'd with much Thankfulness, that in *other Places*, where the Work has greatly flourish'd, there have been few if any of these Disorders and Excesses. But who can wonder, if at such a Time as this Satan should intermingle himself, to hinder and blemish a Work so directly contrary to the Interests of his own Kingdom? Or, if while so much good Seed is showing, *the Enemy should be busy to sow Tares*? We should therefore, in the *Bowels of Jesus*, beseech such as have been Partakers of this Work, or are zealous to promote it, that they *be not ignorant of Satan's Devices*; that they *watch* and *pray* against errors and Misconduct of every Kind, lest they blemish and hinder that which they desire to honour and advance.[16]

Prince also sought to defend and expand the revival by publishing the first evangelical magazine, the *Christian History*. Prince worked with his son, the editor, to put the revival in its historical and global context. They published accounts of earlier colonial revivals and reported news from the British Isles. When the magazine's two-year run concluded in 1745, they bound all 104 issues together as an invaluable record of the awakening.

The *Christian History* walked a fine line between criticizing radical excess and answering skeptics who saw the revival as a whole lot of misguided enthusiasm. They understood the awakening, despite some regrettable elements, to be a sovereign work of God. Even so, historians have assessed the human factors that made the revival plausible in various locales that suddenly exhibited great enthusiasm for the gospel. With the benefit of hindsight, we observe several contributing factors that preceded widespread awakening. This discovery process is similar to how historians assess causes for the Protestant Reformation and biblical scholars explain the advance of Christianity following Jesus' death and resurrection.

Colonial Christians, especially in New England, expected that God occasionally blesses his people with a heightened experience of his grace. They knew what to look for when a revival broke out. They worried that colonial religion had cooled since their forefathers' day, so they felt the need for an awakening. And there was no shortage of pastors who encouraged them to pursue revival, especially through prayer. They may have been surprised when revival did indeed break out, but they were prepared.

Additionally, the constant threat of war with powerful France and Spain between 1688 and 1763 worried colonists who hoped the display of godliness in the revivals would lead God to show mercy and save them from Catholic threats. Roads improved significantly in the early to mid-eighteenth century, enabling itinerant ministers such as Whitefield to traverse the colonies. Faster ships enabled him to play a significant role in revivals as far apart as Georgia and Scotland. Improved mail service allowed the revival's leaders to share the good news and learn from one another. Many new periodicals carried eyewitness reports from far-flung locales. New printing presses published works from Whitefield and Edwards that shaped expectations for revival. All these factors contributed to a climate ripe for revival.

Enduring Effects

The revival had faded in New England by 1745, but not before it permanently altered America. The awakening led to a renewed effort to evangelize Native Americans, an effort that had effectively stopped after King Philip's War several decades earlier. Revival even broke out among the Montauk on Long Island in September 1742. David Brainerd, the student expelled from Yale, visited the revival in February 1743. When he died of tuberculosis in 1747, Brainerd left behind a journal of his experiences as a missionary to Native Americans. His good friend Jonathan Edwards edited and published the journals, which became a best-selling work and inspiration to subsequent generations of missionaries who took the gospel to all corners of the globe.

After Edwards was dismissed as pastor in Northampton in 1750, he moved his family to Stockbridge, Massachusetts, an Indian mission town founded in 1739. He adjusted the content of his highly technical sermons to suit his new audience. He found the Indians receptive to the gospel, even though he grew frustrated by the political scheming among the mission's benefactors. Nevertheless, the new position also afforded him time to complete two of his most famous theological treatises, *Freedom of the Will* and *Original Sin*.

The awakening also transformed African-American attitudes toward Christianity. New Lights, ministers who supported the revival, preached to audiences that included both whites and blacks. Many congregations accepted their first black members. Some slave owners were predictably upset. The *Weekly History* contained an account of a Boston slave owner who walked in on his slave preaching to himself, imitating Whitefield's dramatic style. The owner, no fan of the revival, was so amused that he called together his friends for some after-dinner entertainment.

"Supplying his friends with pipes and glasses all around, he instructed his slave to mount a stool in the center of the room and preach as he had the day before," historian Frank Lambert explains. "As he began, the company laughed heartily, but when he warned against blaspheming the Holy Spirit and proclaimed the necessity of the new birth, 'the Negro spoke with such Authority that struck the Gentlemen to Heart.' To their host's dismay, the men began to listen intently, and many, as a result of that day's 'entertainment,' became 'pious sober Men.'"[17]

The Holy Spirit enjoys such surprises.

NOTES

1. Thomas S. Kidd, *The Great Awakening: The Roots of Evangelical Christianity in Colonial America* (New Haven, Conn.: Yale University Press, 2007), xiv.

2. George M. Marsden, *A Short Life of Jonathan Edwards* (Grand Rapids: Eerdmans, 2008), 60.

3. Jonathan Edwards, "A Divine and Supernatural Light," in *A Jonathan Edwards Reader*, ed. John E. Smith, Harry S. Stout, and Kenneth P. Minkema (New Haven, Conn.: Yale University Press, 1995), 112.

4. Jonathan Edwards, "Sinners in the Hands of an Angry God," in *A Jonathan Edwards Reader*, ed. John E. Smith, Harry S. Stout, and Kenneth P. Minkema (New Haven, Conn.: Yale University Press, 1995), 97–98.

5. Jonathan Edwards, "The Distinguishing Marks of a Work of the Spirit of God," in *Jonathan Edwards on Revival* (Carlisle, Pa.: Banner of Truth Trust, 1965), 106.

6. George Whitefield, *The Nature and Necessity of Our NEW BIRTH in Christ Jesus, in Order to Salvation* (London, 1737).

7. Thomas Prince, *The Christian History: Containing Accounts of the Revival and Progress of the Propagation of Religion in Great Britain and America*, 2 vols. (Boston: 1743–1745): 2:358–59.

8. Walter Isaacson, ed., *A Benjamin Franklin Reader* (New York: Simon and Schuster, 2003), 489.

9. Ibid., 491–92.

10. Marsden, *Short Life of Jonathan Edwards*, 62.

11. Luke Tyerman, *The Life of the Rev. George Whitefield*, 2 vols. (London: Hodder & Stoughton, 1876), 1:428.

12. Michael J. Crawford, "The Spiritual Travels of Nathan Cole," *The William and Mary Quarterly*, 33, no. 1 (January 1976): 92–94.

13. Gilbert Tennent, "The Danger of an Unconverted Ministry" (Philadelphia, 1740).

14. Kidd, *Great Awakening*, 106.

15. Edward Hickman, ed., *The Works of Jonathan Edwards with a Memoir by Sereno E. Dwight*, vol. 1 (Carlisle, Pa.: Banner of Truth Trust, 1974), http://www.ccel.org/ccel/edwards/works1.i.xi.html?highlight=lost%20in%20god#highlight (January 14, 2010).

16. Richard L. Bushman, ed., *The Great Awakening: Documents on the Revival of Religion, 1740–1745* (Chapel Hill: University of North Carolina Press, 1989), 131.

17. Frank Lambert, *Inventing the "Great Awakening"* (Princeton, N.J.: Princeton University Press, 1999), 168.

CHAPTER 3

GOD AND MEN AT YALE

Second Great Awakening, 1790s to 1840s
NORTH AMERICA

In his provocatively titled 1974 book, *Calvinism versus Democracy*, Stephen Berk traces the inception of the Second Great Awakening back to Timothy Dwight, who served Yale College as president from 1795 to 1817. Berk, who taught at California State University in Long Beach, drives a wedge between the revival Dwight enjoyed and the one led by his Puritan grandfather, Jonathan Edwards. "Unlike the earlier Awakening," Berk wrote, "it was not a spontaneous upwelling of faith, but a calculated endeavor, planned and executed by conservative evangelicals."[1] According to Berk, these conservatives planned the revival in order to consolidate clerical control and stamp out the seeds of Jeffersonian democracy creeping into New England from the south. "[Dwight's] immediate concern was the fate of a privileged Federalist-Congregational establishment in Connecticut."[2]

At the end of his preface, however, Berk added an arresting afterword:

> The author wrote this work from the point of view of a non-Christian, [Berk explained]. However, after having submitted it for publication, he experienced conversion to evangelical Christianity, the culmination of a long search for inner peace. While remaining critical of certain human failings in

American revivalistic Protestantism, the author wishes here to affirm its overall spiritual basis. The Awakening which Timothy Dwight led was an honest, though sometimes overheated, Christian response to growing secularism.[3]

Be careful, his example warns, of what you study. It just might change you.

The Second Great Awakening, extending from the 1790s as late as the 1840s, took place in regions such as upstate New York, termed the "Burned-Over District" for an intense series of revivals. Charles Finney, who inspired this term in his 1876 autobiography, conducted evangelistic meetings throughout this section of central and western New York. But Finney was far from the only religious leader who gained a large following in this notorious region. William Miller excited crowds with his promise that Christ would return between March 21, 1843, and March 21, 1844. The Millerite ranks thinned by the time Miller extended Jesus' window of opportunity to October 22. Joseph Smith went public with revelation he said the angel Moroni showed him in western New York in 1827. His band of pioneer Mormons left for Ohio amid mounting opposition in 1830. The Burned-Over District also attracted an eclectic cast of seers who capitalized on the tumultuous times.

The Second Great Awakening started somewhat more calmly. In the 1790s, revivals broke out in a number of churches in Connecticut. But then a rowdy group of settlers out west likewise experienced revival. In 1797 James McGready asked his church members in Logan County, Kentucky, to pray for revival. And if any place needed it, the West did. Drunkenness, fighting, and all sorts of immorality reigned. What could McGready and his church do but pray? For one year they committed to pray half an hour every Saturday evening at dusk, another half hour every Sunday morning, and the full Sabbath every third Sunday of each month. Three years later, McGready reported back to the *New York Missionary Magazine* that he could see the coming crest of revival like a "few scattering floods of salvation."[4]

The scattered floods merged into a torrent in August 1801 with the camp meetings in Cane Ridge, Kentucky. Between 10,000 and

Camp meetings in Cane Ridge, Kentucky, attracted crowds as large as 25,000. (Courtesy of the Disciples of Christ Historical Society.)

25,000 frontier people gathered to hear the gospel and revel in the joyous atmosphere. Washington College president George Baxter visited Kentucky after the revival had erupted and noted dramatic changes in behavior. Remarkably, he heard not a word of swearing from the rough and wild frontiersmen. Instead, religious awe pervaded Kentucky.

Many folks back in the refined East still had their doubts, wondering, perhaps, if any good could come from Kentucky. No matter, the era of eastern dominance in American Christianity was coming to a close. The 1800s would belong to upstart Methodists and Baptists who burned themselves out planting frontier churches. But the established Congregationalists weren't through ... yet. The revival lamp lit by Jonathan Edwards still shone over his old New England haunts.

Dwight's Auspicious Start

Timothy Dwight was born in 1752 in Northampton, Massachusetts, the oldest son of his eponymous father, a wealthy landowner and military officer. His mother, Mary, was Jonathan and Sarah Edwards's third daughter. Their marriage tightened the close bond already shared by the Dwight and Edwards families. Colonel John Dwight, Timothy's grandfather and a pillar of the small Northampton community, had supported Jonathan Edwards during the dispute that cost him his job as pastor and forced the family to leave Northampton.

By all accounts, Timothy Dwight was well liked and extraordinarily intelligent as a child. He combined the social acumen of his father's side with the natural intelligence from his mother's side. It took only one lesson for Mary to teach the alphabet to Timothy. He was reading his favorite part of the Bible, the Old Testament historical books, by the time he was four. Without his parents' permission, Dwight snuck away to read their books. Before anyone had discovered his disobedience, Dwight had taught himself Latin.[5] Like his maternal grandfather, Dwight enrolled at Yale when he was thirteen. But it turns out the Dwight family waited too long to send their eldest son to college. He was bored in New Haven because so much was review for the precocious teenager. And bored students find trouble one way or another. In Dwight's day, the lax Yale administration offered few impediments.

"Thrown suddenly into the midst of so many temptations at the age of thirteen, it is not surprising that he faltered," Dwight biographer Charles Cunningham noted. "Nay, he stumbled badly. He fell, alas, into the vice of card playing. However, he did not reach the bottom of the pit, as did many of his classmates. His mother had trained him so long and so thoroughly in Edwardian ethics that, to his credit, he never actually gambled."[6]

Even if he never gambled, Dwight was neglecting his studies, and his new tutor wouldn't stand to see him waste such giftedness. Stephen Mitchell confronted Dwight with this concern. Chastened but not bowed, Dwight left in a huff. So Mitchell tried another tactic. He called for Dwight and explained how much he could achieve if only he would put forth his best effort. Only help from a classmate had protected Mitchell from making similar mistakes when he was a student. This time Mitchell's approach apparently resonated with Dwight. "He handled the situation with firmness but also with genuine sympathy," Cunningham wrote. "This time he succeeded. No threats, no punishments were necessary. Persuasion accomplished his purpose far more satisfactorily."[7]

Dwight was a changed man his last two years at Yale. Every morning he woke up at 3:30 a.m., one hour before chapel in the spring and fall, to study Greek. But studying by candlelight exacted a physical toll. Over the years, Dwight's eyesight failed, and he suffered from excruciatingly painful headaches. But late in his life, Dwight could still quote Homer from memory.[8]

Infidelity on the Run

When the forty-three-year-old Dwight returned to Yale as president in 1795, he found a situation not unlike the one he imbibed in his first two years as a student. Near the end of the elderly Ezra Stiles's tenure as president, Yale was no bastion for Christian piety. The famed pastor and patriarch Lyman Beecher was a junior at Yale when Dwight replaced the deceased Stiles. Reflecting back on his student days, Beecher remembered the "college was in a most ungodly state." Only about 10 percent of 125 students at the school, which had produced so many of New England's pastoral pillars, would now take the name of Christ in public. The spiritual reticence of the other 90 percent reflected dramatic changes inaugurated by the Revolutionary War, which introduced many Americans to French critiques of religion.

Indeed, with revolution raging across the Atlantic, Dwight and other Christian intellectuals had good reason to worry that the fledgling American republic might embrace the radicalism that ousted the monarchy and church leaders in France. If even upstanding Yale students gravitated toward the Enlightenment's anti-Christian philosophers, who would protect the church?

"The college church was almost extinct," Beecher observed. "Most of the students were skeptical, and rowdies were plenty. Wine and liquors were kept in many rooms; intemperance, profanity, gambling and licentiousness were common. I hardly know how

I escaped," the noted prohibitionist recalled. "That was the day of the infidelity of the Tom Paine school. Boys that dressed flax in the barn, as I used to, read Tom Paine and believed him; I read, and fought him all the way. Never had any propensity to infidelity. But most of the class before me were infidels and called each other Voltaire, Rousseau, D'Alembert, etc. etc."[9]

Fully aware of the challenge, Dwight left a comfortable pastorate in Fairfield, Connecticut, to move to New Haven. Still, the aggressive nature of the apostasy he encountered among Yale students was enough to weaken any pastor's knees. Dwight explained:

> Striplings scarcely found that the world had been enveloped in general darkness through a long succession of preceding ages, and that the light of human wisdom had just begun to dawn upon the human race. The world they resolutely concluded to have been probably eternal, and matter the only existence. Man, they determined, sprang like a mushroom out of the earth like a chemical process; and the power of thinking, choice and motive were merely a result of elective affinities. If, however, there was a God and man was a creative being, he was created only to be happy. As therefore, animal pleasure is the only happiness, so they resolved that the enjoyment of that pleasure is the only end of his creation.[10]

Decades earlier, Dwight's grandfather had tussled with Northampton teenagers he believed wasted their time frivolously, lacking the serious pursuit of godliness that characterizes true Christians. But in one particularly heated dispute over "bad books," Jonathan Edwards's authority eroded, and the community ousted him. If the students could portray Dwight as cold, unsympathetic, and out of touch, they might have convinced friends of Yale to do the same. Dwight, however, immediately set to the work of leading the school with passion and precision. Within the first year, student behavior improved dramatically. He taught regularly as professor of theology, preached every week, and advised seniors. Through this regular interaction, students got to know Dwight personally as a humble, pious role model.

They learned he was also a man of integrity during his first weekly public disputation. The seniors provided Dwight with a list of debate questions, but he selected the one option no one believed he could or would: "Are the Scriptures of the Old and New Testament the word of God?" At the time, denying biblical authority was grounds for dismissal for faculty. But under the influence of European philosophy, the students had begun to doubt Scripture's reliability. They suspected the faculty of fearing a genuine debate over this crucial issue that might expose problems with the Bible and cost them their jobs. By offering this question to Dwight, the seniors dared their new president to test his mettle. By selecting this question, Dwight dared the seniors to mount the best case they could against the Bible.

Dwight promised not to assume the seniors personally believed everything about the arguments they adopted for the purposes of debate. Dwight heard them out, but their points did not catch him by surprise. He had previously published a sermon titled "The Genuineness and Authenticity of the New Testament." When his turn came, Dwight meticulously, ruthlessly demolished their case and constructed a well-reasoned defense of the Bible's accuracy.

"From that moment Infidelity was not only without a stronghold, but without a lurking place," Dwight's son, Sereno, later reported. "To espouse her cause was now as unpopular as before it had been to profess a belief in Christianity. Unable to endure the exposure of argument, she fled from the retreats of learning ashamed and disgraced."[11]

Timothy Dwight ensured that arguments against Christianity would find no safe harbor by preaching six solid months on the question of

Yale students revered their learned, revival-minded president, Timothy Dwight. (From Manuscripts and Archives, Yale University Library.)

biblical authority and accuracy. His 1797 baccalaureate address, "The Nature and Danger of Infidel Philosophy," has been reprinted in several editions. Confident in his abilities, and more importantly in his God, Dwight was not intimidated from tackling challenging topics directly.

"A gentleman once asked me whether I allowed my children to read the books of infidels. I told him yes: for they must become acquainted with them sooner or later, and while I am living I can confute the arguments they use," Dwight explained. "I should be unwilling to have them find these arguments unawares, with nobody to meet them."[12]

Those who were privileged to study with Dwight would never forget the courage he demonstrated by directly engaging the moral and intellectual problems Yale students struggled with as adolescents. He left a strong impression on several of his star pupils. As Beecher recalled:

> To a mind appreciative like mine, his preaching was a continual course of education and a continual feast. He was copious and polished in style, though disciplined and logical. There was a pith and power of doctrine there that has not been since surpassed, if equaled. I took notes of all his discourses, condensing and forming skeletons. He was of noble form, with a noble head and body, and had one of the sweetest smiles that ever you saw. He always met me with a smile. Oh, how I loved him! I loved him as my own soul, and he loved me as a son.... He was universally revered and loved. I never knew but one student undertake to frustrate his wishes.[13]

Revival Reaches Yale

Signs of revival began to emerge as early as 1797, when a group of twenty-five students founded the Moral Society of Yale College. Members of this secret society pledged to hold one another accountable in small groups similar to the Wesleys' Holy Clubs at Oxford. Just one year earlier, only ten students would have publicly professed Christian belief, and eight of them were seniors. As in Dwight's hometown of Northampton more than fifty years earlier, when revival first appeared among the young people who had previously shown little interest in religion, this stirring foreshadowed bigger outpourings to come.

Dwight believed that revivals foreshadowed the time when Jesus would return and reign. He defined revival as times when "considerable" numbers become "subjects of piety" within a brief period. "A Revival of Religion, therefore, means nothing more than that multitudes in a kind of concert, and within a little time, feel and confess its power," Dwight explained.[14] Like his grandfather, Dwight believed only God could send revival. Following the apostle Paul in 1 Corinthians 3:6–7, Dwight borrowed from agricultural imagery to explain how divine agency and human responsibility correspond. A farmer may plant the seeds, but rain and sunshine from the heavens make the plants grow. So also preachers sow the Word, but God alone can make those means effective.

Dwight identified several means other than gospel preaching that God uses to reveal himself. These include Bible reading, prayer, talking with Christians, catechism, and self-examination. Not coincidentally, these are the same means Dwight employed as he promoted revival among Yale students. Yet even this moderate position that held God's absolute sovereignty and his ordinary means of grace in balance did not persuade everyone to support revival. Just as in his grandfather's day, many venerable pastors wanted nothing to do with such outbreaks of religious fervor, no matter how orderly or biblically defensible.

Sounding very much like Edwards, Dwight proceeded to defend revival by explaining that one can't dismiss the concept merely by pointing out cases where things got out of hand.

> Suppose then, that amid much Enthusiasm, and many delusions, there should be some real piety; that among multitudes, who in what is called a Revival of Religion are anxious about their salvation, a single man should become a genuine convert, and actually embrace the offer of eternal life. This, certainly, is

supposing the least; and less, probably, than the truth, in any case of this nature. Would not the salvation of this individual more than balance all the evils, which you apprehend from the Enthusiasm in question?... Would not the arrival even of this one man in the regions of immortality be a source of everlasting joy to the Church of the First-born? Who, unless animated with the spirit of a fiend, can fail to welcome the conversion, from which such glorious consequences will spring, with the most ardent feelings of gratulation![15]

There was sufficient cause for great celebration in 1802 when one-third of the Yale student body, then numbering 230, professed new faith in Christ. Freshman Heman Humphrey remembered the revival as a mighty rushing wind. Humphrey went on to serve Amherst as president from 1824 to 1845. He passed on the Yale legacy to his students and trained ministers in how to seek and discern revival.

The whole college was shaken. It seemed for a time as if the whole mass of the students would press into the kingdom. It was the Lord's doing, and marvelous in all eyes. Oh, what a blessed change!... It was a glorious reformation. It put a new face upon the college. It sent a thrill of joy and thanksgiving far and wide into the hearts of its friends, who had been praying that the waters of salvation might be poured into the fountain from which so many streams were annually sent out.[16]

The revival had begun inconspicuously, with a small band of students meeting weekly over several months to pray that God would visit Yale the way he had been visiting the frontier with revival. The revival seemed to spread rapidly after a well-known senior professed newfound devotion to Christ. A few isolated experiences turned into a clearly discernible trend. By the end of the year, fifty-eight students had joined the college church. Benjamin Silliman, later the college's first chemistry professor, wrote home to tell his mother about the new atmosphere on campus. He described the college as a "little temple" where students delighted in prayer and praise.[17]

The revival left a strong impression on Dwight too. He met with students to pray and hear their confessions. His prayers had been answered, his vision realized as revival spread from student to student. Students who previously hid their faith went public. Others watching from the sidelines began joining the awakening. "Those were memorable days," Dwight remembered.

> Such triumphs of grace, none whose privilege it was to witness them, had ever before seen. So sudden and so great was the change in individuals, and in the general aspect of the college, that those who had been waiting for it were filled with wonder as well as joy, and those who knew not what it meant were awe-struck and amazed. Wherever students were found in their rooms, in the chapel, in the hall, in the college-yard, in their walks about the city, the reigning impression was, "Surely God is in this place." The salvation of the soul was the great subject of thought, of conversation, of absorbing interest; the convictions of many were pungent and overwhelming; the "peace in believing" which succeeded, was not less strongly marked. Yet amidst these overpowering impressions, there was no one, except a single individual, who having resisted former convictions, yielded for a short time to dangerous temptation, in whose conduct any thing of a wild or irrational character appeared.[18]

When the students returned from vacation, Dwight noticed that the revival continued even "stronger and more settled." The number of students transformed had grown from fifty to eighty or more. Even though the revival fires eventually flickered out, the awakening left a long legacy at Yale and beyond. Thirty students—half the revived senior class—entered pastoral ministry. In the next four years after the 1802 revival, a total of sixty-nine graduates went on to serve in local churches. In the previous four years before the revival, a mere thirteen graduates had become pastors.[19] Men like Beecher would become the rising generation's most influential pulpiteers.

Revival Strikes Again

By 1808 Yale had lost most of the religious fervor that characterized the students in 1802. Only small groups of Christian disciples held out against the pervasive worldliness in the school. Yet the surrounding community buzzed with revival. This distressing contrast burdened President Dwight. Normally Dwight spoke with a dynamic style more typical of the early 1800s than of his grandfather, who read his dense manuscripts. Because of his faltering eyesight, Dwight could not rely on notes, so he was free to engage with his audience. But one night during evening prayers, Dwight's demeanor suddenly changed.

"The chapter was read with an altered tone; the hymn was recited with a faltering accent; and when he joined the choir, as was his custom, his usually loud and sonorous voice became weak and tremulous. He sung but a single stanza and stopped," remembered Chauncey Goodrich, a student at the time. He later pastored Park Street Church in Boston before returning to Yale as a rhetoric professor from 1818 to 1838.

> Next came the prayer. President Dwight was always remarkable for humility of manner in prayer. Even when his lofty mind rose amid the inspirations of a near approach to God, and his language became, as it often became on such occasions, sublime, he was always humble and abased. But on that evening, it seemed as if the subduing power of the gospel was doubly upon him. There was such an apparent coming down — such an obvious holy prostration of the soul, as indicated that the Spirit of God was with him. He spake as if "dust and ashes" were addressing the Eternal on his throne. The burden of his prayer was, "an acknowledgement of the sovereignty of God in the dispensations of his grace." And yet he made that solemn truth the foundation of one of the most appropriate arguments ever presented to a throne of mercy for a revival of religion. Never did a minister plead more fervently for his people — never a father more importunately for his children, than he did for his pupils before him. Nor were the wants of the churches, nor the influence of a revival in the college upon the Redeemer's kingdom in the land — in the world, forgotten.[20]

The next day, Dwight preached from Luke 7:11–15 about the recently deceased young man from Nain whom Jesus resurrected with the stirring command, "Young man, I say unto thee, arise!" Yale students would need such a miracle to escape the college's spiritual malaise, Dwight warned. He compared the spiritual state of Yale students to the young man as he was being carried away. Whether they realized it or not, they were spiritually dead in their sins and needed resurrection power.

> By this I intend, that *all such youths are impenitent, unbelieving, sinners*. It is not here intended, merely, that you are impenitent and unbelieving. It is further intended, that *you are permanently of this character*; that you are fixed, and obstinate; that you have a hard heart, and a blind mind; a heart hard, a mind blind, in its very nature.... You are not *casually* sinners; yielding to sudden and powerful temptation, in the weak, unguarded hour, and in circumstances peculiarly dangerous. You are *sinners of design*; of contrivance; with premeditation; from habit; and without mixture. Do you receive this charge as untrue, as unkind, or even as doubtful? Look back, I beseech you, upon the whole course of your lives; and tell me, if you can remember a single day, in which you have faithfully obeyed *God*, believed in the Redeemer, or repented of your sins.[21]

But Dwight did not abandon his hearers in their sins. He brought them to the foot of the Cross where they could behold Jesus.

> He died, with the complete foreknowledge of all the guilty and grossness which I have rehearsed: yet he died. The Spirit of Grace began to strive, with the same foreknowledge of the same guilt. Still he strives with you. Still with a voice, sweeter than that of angels, he whispers to you daily, "Turn ye, turn ye, why will ye die?" It is, therefore, no unreasonable thing to hope, that, notwithstanding the blessings which you have abused, have been very great, notwithstanding your sins are of no common dye, Christ may still extend mercy to some of your number; and may say to one, and another, "Young man, arise."[22]

Indeed, revival spread calmly from student to student over the next few weeks. This outbreak was characterized by introspection rather than emotional outbursts. When offering spiritual counsel to students, Dwight was careful not to interject his own opinion of whether true spiritual transformation had taken place. Rather, he asked whether the young man was prepared to serve God. He had recognized the tendency of emotional awakenings to swing from exuberant joy one minute to grave doubt the next. So he looked for evidence of conversion in daily living, rather than in private spirituality alone. Genuine religion transforms the whole person, Dwight believed. True Christians show kindness, walk humbly, deal honestly, and give generously.

A third revival affecting 180 students broke out during the 1812–13 school year after a few faithful Christians had committed to praying together.[23] They identified one student, senior Elias Cornelius, whom they expected would oppose the revival. But after praying for Cornelius, he joined the revival and led almost twenty of his fellow students to the Lord before graduation. He later studied theology with Dwight. During this time, the winter of 1814–15, he convened a small band who awoke before 3:30 a.m. on Sundays to pray for revival. The students would remember these times among the happiest of their lives. Their prayers were answered when God sent an especially emotional fourth revival in April 1815. The response was so dramatic that the students petitioned Dwight to suspend classes so they could spend all their time enjoying the fruit of revival. Dwight declined, because he did not think revival should cause the students to neglect their normal course of study. Perhaps he also discerned that the revival might soon cease, which indeed it did. Taking after his grandfather, Dwight privileged the role of affections, or inclinations, in revival. But he cautioned that emotion alone is no sure sign of awakening. Such a work of God among students would lead to devotion to God's Word, studies, and loving their neighbors.

Dwight's Lasting Legacy

Dwight's measured response illustrates the value of discretion in his role as a spiritual and educational leader. Dwight faithfully preached the gospel during regular sermons, but he also developed a more explicitly evangelical curriculum for Yale. He counseled and prayed with the small groups of students God always seemed to raise up to begin plowing the soil for revival. He could overwhelm students with his superior intellect, as he did to defend the authority of Scripture. More often, he built trust with students by showing that he cared about them and believed in them. He wore down his body helping students become world-class scholars. But students understood that Dwight wanted nothing more than for them to inherit eternal life by trusting in Jesus Christ.

Dwight served as president until 1817, when he died of prostate cancer. It would be impossible to adequately describe the legacy he left behind at Yale and beyond. Revival spread from Yale to Dartmouth and Princeton, though Harvard continued its slide toward Unitarianism. Yale continued to experience revival long after Dwight's death. The largest revival came in 1831, when 104 students became members of the college church, and 900 others in New Haven were converted.[24] In 1858, the same year star Dwight pupil and Yale Divinity School theology professor Nathaniel Taylor died, revival returned to the school amid a powerful national awakening. Dwight would have appreciated the revival's reliance on prayer, rather than special preachers or services. Continuing through the twentieth century, colleges were fertile soil for revival as young believers covenanted together in prayer and publicly confessed their sins. The revivals Dwight witnessed at Yale would be reprised in places such as Asbury and Wheaton with students who hungered for a vision of God in his holiness and grace.

Dwight even managed to leave his mark on popular hymnody. He had written marching songs for the Continental Army during his one-year stint as chaplain for the First Connecticut Brigade near the beginning of the Revolutionary War. But his first love was Christ's church, as evidenced in his hymn "I Love Thy Kingdom, Lord!"

I love Thy kingdom, Lord!
    The house of Thine abode—
The Church our blest Redeemer
    saved with His own precious blood.

I love Thy Church, O God!
   Her walls before Thee stand,
dear as the apple of Thine eye
   and graven on Thy hand.

Beyond my highest joy
   I prize her heav'nly ways —
Her sweet communion, solemn vows,
   her hymns of love and praise.

Sure as Thy truth shall last,
   to Zion shall be giv'n
the brightest glories earth can yield,
   and brighter bliss of heav'n.

"A brighter bliss of heav'n" is what Dwight longed to experience in revival. As a farmer, pastor, professor, and college president, Dwight ached because of the chasm of sin that separates us from God. In revival, the church catches a fleeting glimpse of God's everlasting kingdom, when the believer will be finally renewed according to the image of the Creator (Col. 3:10).

NOTES

1. Stephen E. Berk, *Calvinism versus Democracy: Timothy Dwight and the Origins of American Evangelical Orthodoxy* (New Haven, Conn.: Archon, 1974), x.

2. Ibid., xi.

3. Ibid., xii.

4. John D. Woodbridge, Mark A. Noll, and Nathan O. Hatch, *The Gospel in America: Themes in the Story of America's Evangelicals* (Grand Rapids: Zondervan, 1979), 142.

5. Charles E. Cunningham, *Timothy Dwight, 1752–1817: A Biography* (New York: Macmillan, 1942), 15.

6. Ibid., 23.

7. Ibid., 25–26.

8. Ibid., 26–27.

9. Lyman Beecher, *The Autobiography of Lyman Beecher*, ed. Barbara M. Cross (Cambridge, Mass.: Harvard University Press, 1961), 1:27.

10. Timothy Dwight, *Travels in New England and New York* (London: William Baynes and Son, Ogle, Duncan & Co., 1823), 4:364–65.

11. Timothy Dwight, *Theology Explained and Defended in a Series of Sermons* (New Haven, Conn.: Converse, 1823), 23.

12. Cited in Cunningham, *Timothy Dwight*, 304.

13. Beecher, *Autobiography*, 1:27.

14. Timothy Dwight, "On Revivals of Religion," in *Sermons* (New Haven, Conn.: Hezekiah Howe and Durrie & Peck, 1828), 1:234.

15. Ibid., 1:239–40.

16. Heman Humphrey, *Revival Sketches and Manual* (New York: American Tract Society, 1859), 198.

17. Charles R. Keller, *The Second Great Awakening in Connecticut* (New Haven, Conn.: Yale University Press, 1942), 42.

18. Chauncey A. Goodrich, "Narrative of Revivals of Religion in Yale College," *American Quarterly Register* 10 (February 1838): 295–96.

19. Humphrey, *Revival Sketches and Manual*, 198.

20. Goodrich, "Narrative of Revivals of Religion in Yale College," 297–98.

21. Timothy Dwight, "The Youth of Nain," in *Sermons* (New Haven, Conn.: Hezekiah Howe and Durrie & Peck, 1828), 2:186–87.

22. Ibid., 2:193.

23. Earle E. Cairns, *An Endless Line of Splendor: Revivals and Their Leaders from the Great Awakening to the Present* (Wheaton, Ill.: Tyndale, 1986), 92.

24. James B. Reynolds, Samuel H. Fisher, and Henry B. Wright, eds., *Two Centuries of Christian Activity at Yale* (New York: Putnam, 1901), 83.

CHAPTER 4

WHEN BUSINESSMEN PRAY

Prayer Meeting Revival, 1857 to 1858
NORTH AMERICA

When Billy Graham preached to 250,000 in New York City's Central Park on September 22, 1991, crusade organizers proudly noted the date. The event fell one day earlier than the anniversary of Jeremiah Lanphier's first prayer meeting at New York's Fulton Street Church in 1857.[1] This wasn't the first time Graham and his team commemorated that awakening. Surely it was no coincidence that Graham had convened his first, long-awaited New York City crusade in 1957, one century after prayer meetings around the country eventually erupted in revival. Martyn Lloyd-Jones had this awakening in mind when he selected 1957 as the year he delivered a series of sermons on revival.

These historically minded evangelists commemorated the 1857–58 revival for good reason. It was "perhaps the closest thing to a truly national revival in American history," according to historian Kathryn Long. Every Protestant denomination was caught up in its wake. Lanphier's prayer meetings merely attracted the most media attention. The revival spread from coast to coast and even continued across the Atlantic after the fervor began to wane in America.[2] Between 1856 and 1859, Protestant denominations added 474,000 members. Methodists and Baptists led the way, accounting for more than three-fourths of these new members.[3]

J. Edwin Orr's recount of the revival, titled *The Event of the Century*, borrows the descriptor from noted Harvard historian Perry Miller. This was the century that also included the Civil War. Nevertheless, the hyperbole captures the influence and scope of this revival that has somehow slipped out of popular evangelical remembrance. Orr observed:

> The influences of this awakening were felt everywhere in the country. It not only captured the big cities, but it also spread through every town, village, and country hamlet. It also swamped schools and colleges and it affected classes regardless of condition. As a divine influence seemed to pervade the country, the hearts of men were strangely warmed by a power outpoured in unusual ways. Lacking all fanaticism, there was an unusual unanimity of approval by religious and secular observers, with scarcely a critical voice heard anywhere. The fruits of Pentecost were repeated three hundred-fold in the population of thirty million.[4]

Nestled between the Second Great Awakening and the Civil War, the so-called Prayer Meeting or Businessmen's Revival of 1857–58 has often been overshadowed. But closer examination reveals a revival worth remembering and repeating.

Prayers Answered

The years leading up to the Civil War in the mid-nineteenth century were tumultuous, to say the least. Religious fervor had declined from its peak during the long-lasting, multifaceted Second Great Awakening. Church growth was no longer keeping pace with American population growth. The population increased sharply between 1840 and 1860, jumping 35 percent from more than 23 million to beyond 31 million. For the first time, the United States was more populous than the United Kingdom. Much of this growth came from Roman Catholic immigrants, who further reshaped the American religious scene that had been so recently reordered by the earlier awakening. Gang riots in New York City on the Fourth of July in 1857 confirmed to many Protestants that they could not trust these predominantly Italian and Irish immigrants.

The plight of nearly 4 million slaves in America incited extreme emotions on both sides. On March 6, 1857, the Supreme Court handed down one of its most notorious decisions in the Dred Scott case. The court ruled that African-American slaves and their descendants could not be U.S. citizens. In the 1840s, several major denominations split over issues related to slavery, with all sides mustering Bible verses for support. When the churches divided, the nation lost one of its last, best chances of avoiding a cataclysmic conflict. Financial woes added to the already overwhelming sense of dread in the country. The stock market crashed on October 10, 1857. Land speculation, especially by the rapidly expanding railroads, had created the need for a market correction. Banks in Chicago and Philadelphia failed. Then on October 13, 1857, a bank run in New York City crippled the financial system. The Boston banks failed shortly thereafter. Ministers and even journalists believed the collapse was divine judgment against their most worrisome social sins.

"Just then, in the summer of 1857, God interposed in a way which but few if any would have chosen or thought of," Amherst College president Heman Humphrey remembered.

> When men were saying, "Soul, thou hast much goods laid up for many years; take thine ease, eat, drink, and be merry"; when they were building their castles in the air, not easy to be numbered; when the common talk on change was of hundreds of thousands and millions; when, in short, all were saying, "Tomorrow shall be as this day, and more abundant," then suddenly came the crash, as if thunders from a clear sky had simultaneously broken over the whole land. Like a yawning earthquake, it shook down the palaces of the rich, no less than the humble dwellings of the poor, and swallowed up their substance. Men went to bed dreaming all night of their hoarded treasures, and woke up in the morning hopeless bankrupts.[5]

Yet these losses made businessmen more open to revival, Humphrey believed. Many historians today share Humphrey's interpretation of the revival's connection to the financial panic. "Businessmen had both the time and motivation to pray," Kathryn Long said about the panic's practical effects.[6] So echoed a *Christian History* article that regarded financial panic as the revival's catalyst.[7]

But was it really? The same article notes that during the summer of 1857, before Wall Street tanked, Holiness revivalists Walter and Phoebe Palmer traveled throughout Canada and New York speaking before large audiences during camp meetings. Most revival accounts focus narrowly on New York City, for the simple reason of preserving a manageable research scope. So even though not every city took its cues from New York, books often leave this impression. This approach makes for a neat, clean-cut narrative, but it does not account for the local outbreaks before the revival or in cities relatively unaffected by the financial distress. Historically speaking, there is no reason to demand a causation link. God may choose to bring revival out of human calamity. But he need not, and often has not. Not every moment of acute human weakness has led to revival, and several revivals have emerged from self-confident societies.

Revivals are also easier to explain when the Spirit's movement seems to coalesce behind at least one dynamic leader. The closest we come to a unifying figure in the revival of 1857 and 1858 is Jeremiah Calvin Lanphier. But we don't know a great deal about Lanphier. Born in 1809, he left his small town as a young adult to pursue business ventures in the big city, like so many of his contemporaries. He was converted in 1842 at Charles Finney's Broadway Tabernacle in Lower Manhattan. After Lanphier worked twenty years in business, the North Dutch Church at the corner of William and Fulton Streets hired him as a local missionary. As the middle-class neighborhood was giving way to businesses and poor immigrants, the church—located just a five-minute walk to Wall Street and one and a half blocks from Broadway—did not want to move, even though members had been trickling away. With no wife or children, Lanphier spent himself evangelizing the lower classes.

Lanphier hardly produced eye-opening results, but he had an inspired idea. He would invite businessmen to a lunch-hour prayer meeting. Yet the idea seemed anything but inspired when no one arrived for the first half hour on September 23, 1857. Eventually, six men showed up to the North Dutch Church's third-floor classroom and prayed with Lanphier. The next week, twenty turned out. In early October, more than thirty businessmen prayed during their breaks. By that point, they needed a bigger room. Lanphier began seeking coverage of the prayer meetings from religious papers on October 23. The *New York Observer* took note of the meetings on November 5, 1857.

The meeting is begun at twelve o'clock precisely, and it closes exactly on the hour [1:00 p.m.]. The room is full and crowded, and the interest appears to increase from day to day. It began with a modest meeting held once in the week. But the attendance and benefit seemed to demand the more frequent observance of the privilege: now it has become a daily service. With the pressure came a larger attendance and a more spirited service. The probability is that the meeting will be adjourned to the church. Any one comes in or goes out as he pleases. It is the rule of the place to leave at any moment. All sects are here: the formal, state Churchman and the impulsive Methodist who cannot suppress his groan and his "amen"; the sober, substantial Dutchman and the ardent Congregationalist, with all Yankee restlessness on his face; the Baptist and the Presbyterian, joining in the same chorus and bowing at the same altar. Not one woman is in the meeting, the singing from 200 male voices is really majestic.[8]

> **Brethren are earnestly requested to adhere to the 5 minute rule.**

> **PRAYERS & EXHORTATIONS Not to exceed 5 minutes,** *in order to give all an opportunity.* *NOT MORE than 2 CONSECUTIVE* **PRAYERS OR EXHORTATIONS. NO CONTROVERTED POINTS *— DISCUSSED.—***

Each meeting opened with the group singing three to five verses from a hymn. Then someone led in prayer, read Scripture, and opened the floor for prayer requests. Signs set the ground rules: "No Controverted Points Discussed," "Prayers

Rules for the Fulton Street prayer meetings kept participants on topic and on time. (Used by permission of Michael McClymond.)

and Exhortations not to exceed five minutes," and "Not more than two consecutive prayers or exhortations."[9] Businessmen could come and go as they pleased, according to their schedules. Five minutes before 1:00 p.m., they sang a closing hymn, then a pastor delivered a benediction.[10]

Elsewhere in New York City unrelated prayer meetings were taking place. Yet when other cities began to follow New York's example, Lanphier, the unknown evangelist, suddenly became a widely admired figure. Samuel Prime, who documented the revival's progress, described Lanphier as

> tall, well made, with a remarkably pleasant, benevolent face; affectionate in his disposition and manner, possessed of indomitable energy and perseverance, having good musical attainments; gifted in prayer and exhortation to a remarkable degree; modest in his demeanor, ardent in his piety, sound in his judgment; having good common sense, a thorough knowledge of human nature, and those traits of character that make him a welcome guest in any house. He is intelligent, and eminently fitted for the position which he has been called to occupy, which up to the present moment he has so worthily filled.[11]

By focusing narrowly on lay-led prayer meetings, Lanphier cut against contemporary thinking about how to promote revival. Finney's "new measures" did not play a major role in this new awakening. Prime observed the lack of anxious seats and revival machinery.[12] Finney's innovations had divided evangelicals who debated their biblical warrant. But Princeton-trained Presbyterians such as Prime expressed few reservations about working across denominations during this unexpected outbreak of religious interest. The prayer meetings continued into 1858, drawing in James Waddel Alexander, a New York pastor and son of the renowned Princeton Theological Seminary professor Archibald Alexander. "The uptown prayer meetings are very sober and edifying," James Waddel Alexander wrote on April 2.

> I am told the general tendency in all is to increased decorum. The openness of thousands to doctrine, reproof etc., is

undeniable. Our lecture is crowded unendurably—many going away. The publisher of [London preacher Charles] Spurgeon's sermons, says he has sold a hundred thousand. All booksellers agree, that while general trade is down, they never sold so many religious books. You may rest assured there is a great awakening among us, of which not one word gets into the papers; and that there are meetings of great size, as free from irreverence as any you ever saw. I have never seen sacramental occasions more tender and still than some meetings held daily in our part of the town. The best token I have seen of revival was our meeting of Presbytery. I never was at such a one. Brethren seemed flowing together in love, and reported a great increase of attention in all their churches—and this within a very few days. The inquiring condition among ourselves is strange, and all but universal; God grant it may be continued or exchanged for true grace in them all.[13]

By the time Alexander wrote this letter, the revival had grown to include 10,000 praying daily.[14] The newspapers took notice of the startling response from Wall Street's money-minded movers and shakers. The press ate up news of celebrity converts, including boxer Orville "Awful" Gardner. In April 1858, Horace Greeley's *New York Tribune* issued a special revival issue. Journalists analyzed the revival largely in terms they could understand and identify. They reported the number of conversions, described the meetings as orderly, and observed the unity of denominations. Thanks to the New York media's influence and a national telegraph service, the world was soon treated to frequent updates of this remarkable revival.[15]

A National Event

Even Boston, home to several opponents of the First Great Awakening, had caught the revival spirit. The *Christian Watchman and Reflector* reported a new tone and tearful interest overtaking the city. Police officers jaded by violence and strife were shocked to see an outbreak of joy and goodwill among the uneducated and poor, black and white together.[16] In Springfield, Massachusetts, the *Republican* reported orderly meetings where men and women joined together to offer simple prayers and sing boisterous hymns. Some left the meetings with a serious demeanor while others departed in excitement.[17]

Shortly after the bank crash, there was little evidence of revival in hard-hit Philadelphia. A religious and ethnic melting pot since the colonial days, Philadelphia endured violent rivalries between free blacks, working-class Irishmen, and German speakers competing for work.[18] But as the prayers for national revival continued in New York, Philadelphia's prayer meetings grew to 3,000 by March 10.[19] In March and April, firefighters notorious for brawling with one another opened their halls to evangelists. Philadelphians were such grateful participants in the revival that a committee of fifteen members published an account in 1859 called *Pentecost or The Work of God in Philadelphia.* They represented denominations that didn't always get along, including Protestant Episcopalians, New School Presbyterians, Reformed Presbyterians, German Reformed, Associate Presbyterians, Baptists, Old School Presbyterians, Methodist Episcopalians, Reformed Dutch, Society of Friends, Disciples of Christ, Methodist Protestants, Lutherans, and Moravians. They published the recount under the auspices of the Young Men's Christian Association, established in Philadelphia in 1854.

With this book, the committee set out to recognize God's work among them and share the news with the world. They wrote in the preface, "To enter on their work with 'a single eye,' to collect *authentic facts*, to let these facts speak for themselves alike to the intelligent Christian and the candid man of the world, this, and this only, has been their aim."[20] They noted that before God pours out his Spirit in revival, he grants a spirit of heartfelt petition. "God leads his people to pray for that which he designs to give."[21] The churches began to fill in 1857, and a spirit of Christian union accompanied prayer. Preachers shared their pulpits across denominational lines to demonstrate that Christians are not defined by how they disagree but by the beliefs and historical events that unite them. In the spirit of the times, they appealed to the analogy of many states but one nation united.[22] Searching history for models, they settled on the Reformation and First Great Awakening.

The first union prayer meeting was held on November 23, 1857, at the Methodist Episcopal Union Church, a site visited by George Whitefield and built for traveling revival preachers.[23] At first the response was tepid, averaging twelve believers, never exceeding thirty-six. Yet after they moved locations, 300 showed up on Monday, March 8. Suddenly they needed a bigger room, so they secured a hall two days later that seated 2,500 but could fit 4,000 total with the galleries open. When even this arrangement failed to contain the crowds, they opened the hall to the elements. As in New York, anyone could pray or speak for five minutes. A bell was rung when someone exceeded the time limit.

"No man there, no man perhaps, living or dead, has ever seen anything like it," the committee reported. "On the day of Pentecost, Peter preached; Luther preached, and Livingston, and Whitefield and Wesley! Great spiritual movements have usually identified with some eloquent voice; but NO NAME, except the name that is above every name, is identified with this meeting."[24] Indeed, reports of conversion came in from all corners of the city as several public halls opened their doors for meetings. Prayers poured out for others not yet touched by God's grace.

One of the revival's most dynamic leaders was Dudley Tyng, a twenty-nine-year-old Episcopalian. More than 5,000 turned out to hear him preach over the noon hour at the downtown YMCA on March 30, 1858. He preached from Exodus 10:11, "Ye that are men, go and serve the Lord." More than 1,000 heeded the call to follow Christ delivered by the fervent speaker. "I must tell my Master's errand, and I would rather that this right arm were amputated at the trunk than that I should come short of my duty to you in delivering God's message," Tyng told the men.

The words proved tragically prophetic. As he visited a farm the next week, Tyng caught his shirtsleeve in a corn threshing machine. He suffered a deep laceration and died from massive blood loss due to a severed artery. As he died surrounded by other ministers and friends, he told them weakly, "Let us all stand up for Jesus."

Philadelphia's evangelical clergy officiated his funeral together on April 22. George Duffield, pastor of Temple Presbyterian Church, delivered a poetic tribute to Tyng based on his dying words, which became the YMCA motto.

> Stand up, stand up for Jesus; ye soldiers of the cross;
> Lift high His royal banner—it must not suffer loss.
> From vict'ry unto vict'ry His army shall He lead,
> 'Til ev'ry foe is vanquished and Christ is Lord indeed....
>
> Stand up, stand up for Jesus; the trumpet call obey;
> Forth to the mighty conflict in this His glorious day.
> Ye that are men now serve Him against unnumbered foes;
> Let courage rise with danger and strength to strength
>   oppose....
>
> Stand up, stand up for Jesus; the strife will not be long;
> This day the noise of battle—the next, the victor's song.
> To Him that overcometh a crown of life shall be;
> He with the King of Glory shall reign eternally.[25]

The life and death of Tyng show how the revival had united the churches and burdened Christians with passion to introduce the lost to Jesus Christ. The organizers of the prayer meetings solicited requests for unsaved family members and distributed evangelistic tracts as people exited. "By conversing with a friend, by inviting him to a Christian minister, by giving him a book or tract—above all by making him the special subject of prayer in secret, simple as these means appear, they have been all-powerful through the blessing of God to produce the desired result," the committee noted.[26] The committee report closed with an appeal for readers not to delay their salvation, for no one knows what tomorrow will bring. They also challenged anyone to step forward with an explanation for the revival that rejected their belief that God had done it.

> In view of these and a multitude of similar facts, of which these stand only as the imperfect representatives, we feel bound in all honor and conscience, both as men and as Christians, to express to our city, our commonwealth, our country, and the

world at large, our most solemn and undoubting belief, that this last year in the religious history of Philadelphia has been "a year of the right hand of the Most High," and that many of its days have been days of Pentecost indeed. The great question is, "WHAT HATH GOD WROUGHT?" and not "What has been done by man?"[27]

Hitting the Heartland

The revival was certainly not limited to the Northeast. It had spread through the Midwest, in part because a group of conservative Presbyterians rallied in Pittsburgh on December 1, 1857, then issued a letter to congregations urging prayer and preaching for revival.[28] The governor of Ohio induced tears when he told those gathered at a Columbus prayer meeting about his conversion.[29] In Cleveland, 2,000 met daily for prayer.[30] One correspondent in Iowa wrote to New England editors in the spring of 1858 about the revival's reach: "Just as the winds of heaven speak the strongest over the broad open prairies, so some of the prairies, the wind of the Spirit has spoken with an irresistible power, and the sinner in the humblest isolated cabin has rejoiced in a new life."[31]

A similarly enthusiastic report about the awakening's grand scale issued from Appleton, Wisconsin.

> The "Grand Revival" is becoming a universal thing throughout the Union. All our exchanges from those ponderous city dailies down to the smallest of country weeklies, fill their columns to overflowing with accounts of "revivals," "business men's meetings," "protracted meetings," &c., which feature we are glad to behold in all of them. The excitement has spread from city to city, and from village to village; and we hope it may continue to spread from place to place, and from country to country, until the whole world is following in "the narrow path." Let the work go on.[32]

The Midwest's most prominent city seemed unlikely to heed the revival, however. The 1860 census would count 109,620 residents in Chicago. A mere seventy churches sought to meet their spiritual needs. By contrast, a hundred brothels sought to meet the physical lusts of stockyard salesmen and traveling businessmen. Given the difficulty of reaching these men, Dwight L. Moody started a Sunday school class and invited kids off the street near the present-day site of Moody Bible Institute.[33] During the revival, Sunday schools across the nation thrived. Their ranks had grown to more than 11,000 in 1857.[34] The innovation reflected demographic changes. As of 1850, more than half of white Americans were younger than twenty years old. To meet the growing need, *Hymns of the Church Militant* editor Anna Warner wrote a tune first published in 1859 that would become closely linked to Sunday schools ever since.

> Jesus loves me, this I know,
> For the Bible tells me so;
> Little ones to Him belong;
> They are weak, but He is strong.

Despite Chicago's rough reputation, the revival spread much like it did in Philadelphia, with order and denominational unity. The Metropolitan Theater filled with 2,000 praying daily.[35] As in other cities, the mainstream newspapers took notice. We must not mistakenly assume that newspapers at the time commonly reported religious news. Like now, churches rarely garnered more than a brief mention. Media simply could not ignore the big story.

"Writing from a news point, the prominent topic of thought and conversation in Chicago in our streets, in our places of business and in our homes, the subject of the religious awakening now in progress in this community is all absorbing," the *Chicago Daily Press* reported. "It is upon the lips of Christians and of unbelievers. There are few or no scoffers, few who sneer publicly and openly at what is transpiring without excitement, without noise, and cannot be called fanaticism."[36] The *Chicago Daily Democrat* reported likewise. Men and women from all walks of life grew in godliness.[37]

As long as he lived, Moody remained impressed with the pervasive scope of the national revival in 1857 and 1858. Working for the YMCA, organized in Chicago in 1858, Moody observed how Christians linked arms in common cause. His urban evangelistic campaigns between 1875 and 1878 attempted to capture this spirit. Facing death in 1899, Moody said, "I would like before I go hence, to see the whole Church of Christ quickened as it was in 1857, and a wave going from Maine to California that will sweep thousands into the kingdom of God."[38]

Campuses Catch the Revival Fervor

Similar to the Second Great Awakening, college campuses around the country erupted with revival. With administration support, the YMCA and Student Christian Association joined forces at the University of Michigan in Ann Arbor to promote revival.[39] Future temperance leader Frances Willard suppressed her doubts and stepped up to the altar during the revival fervor of 1859 that gripped the North Western Female College in Evanston, Illinois.[40] All told, as many as ninety college revivals swept through American campuses between 1857 and 1859. Those schools included Amherst; the University of California, Berkeley; Dartmouth; Davidson; Oberlin; the University of Pennsylvania; the University of Wisconsin; and Wake Forest.

In some cases, the national revival at the close of the 1850s built upon earlier local outbreaks. John Broadus became a founding professor of New Testament and preaching at the Southern Baptist Theological Seminary in 1859. But earlier that decade, he served as pastor of Charlottesville Baptist Church, then as chaplain for the University of Virginia. When revival broke out in Charlottesville in 1852, he wrote about the events for the *Religious Herald*. Previously, the unconverted showed scant interest in Christianity, and even the Christians lacked fervor. Broadus and others believed nothing but prayer for God's intervention could bring revival from malaise. Women especially responded to the call for fasting and early morning prayer.[41] The petitions seemed to loose the first stirring of revival, because as Broadus preached that fall, he found the congregation more attentive and serious.[42] In October, Broadus's uncle, a well-known Northern Virginia preacher, responded to an invitation to speak in Charlottesville. He stayed only five days, but morning prayer and evening meetings continued until November 5. In all, forty new believers professed faith, and twenty-three sought baptism. Broadus wasn't the agent used to incite revival, but he nevertheless enjoyed how God answered their prayers. "Our meetings were very quiet and solemn; and there was frequently felt a realizing sense of the Divine presence, which could not but impress the heart," Broadus reported. "Especially did we find such pervading solemnity in the sunrise prayer meeting. The number of persons professing conversion is considered large for this place."[43]

When Broadus took a leave of absence from his church to become the university chaplain in 1855, he grew discouraged that the students showed few signs of revival. But as a responsible shepherd of souls, Broadus still kept close tabs on the students' religious progress.

> I know of some eight students who have professed conversion during the session; three in connection with the Baptist meetings; three with the Presbyterians; and two without any special influences. I have taken great pains to ascertain the exact number of religious students, which has never been done before. Thus far, I know of about ninety-five (it will probably reach one hundred) distributed, as nearly as I recollect, (the list not being before me) as follows: Baptists, thirty-six; Presbyterians, twenty-seven; Methodists, eighteen; Episcopal, ten; other denominations, four.[44]

He would have to wait until 1858, the tail end of the national awakening, to see revival again in Charlottesville. To be sure, there had been examples of Christian charity during the intervening years. Prayer meetings still attracted some interest. Students aspiring to the ministry preached in the impoverished countryside and the poor house. But these efforts lacked coordination and focus. Then the campus was demoralized with an outbreak of typhoid that killed twenty students. Amid depression, the community pulled together and revival flared again. The YMCA, operating for one of the first times in conjunction with a university, helped coordinate the revival among several denominations. Church, university, and parachurch worked together in common cause. About 200 students participated in weekly prayer meetings. At least fifty taught Sunday school in Charlottesville or led Bible classes for the college. The YMCA president spent Sunday afternoons teaching slaves about Christianity.[45]

Neither Broadus nor anyone else quite anticipated the greatest legacy emerging from Charlottesville during this time. Broadus and other leading Virginia Baptists had taken the bold step to offer equal if separate education for women by launching the Albemarle Female Institute in Charlottesville. The school offered the same degrees, teaching, tests, and classes as the University of Virginia.

Broadus expressed his pride in the school in a July 1857 letter: "Our Female Institute in Charlottesville has now very encouraging prospects. It did much more than I had expected, amid all the difficulties of a first session. The instruction is more thorough, as well as more extensive in each particular subject, than in any other female school with which I am acquainted."[46]

During the revival in December 1858, Broadus convened evangelistic meetings for the male and female students in town. The Albemarle women prayed for one student they figured would never

Once a skeptic, Lottie Moon inspired Southern Baptists by spending her life as a missionary to China. (Photo courtesy of the International Mission Board.)

show. To their shock, Lottie Moon did indeed attend the meetings. She even spoke privately with Broadus. Moon professed faith on December 21 in the Baptist church, and explained her conversion the next day after applying for membership. "She mentioned that on the night before the inquiry meeting, she had been prevented from sleeping by the barking of a dog. While lying awake, she at last considered the condition of her own soul and determined to give the subject of Christianity an honest, intelligent investigation. Lottie went to the revival meeting to scoff, but returned to pray all night." Her immediate and drastic conversion was evident to friends. One wrote, "She had always wielded an influence because of her intellectual power. Now her great talent was directed into another channel. She immediately took a stand as a Christian." A born leader, Moon began conducting prayer meetings and explaining Scripture to fellow students.[47]

Broadus naturally followed up his evangelism during the revival with a call for students to consider spending their lives as missionaries or pastors. He may not have expected that a woman would be the most famous student to respond. Broadus clearly had high regard for Moon, calling her "the most educated (or cultured) woman in the South." And his was not an isolated observation. A classmate said, "She has a mind and a wealth of knowledge that is the fortune of few women to possess."[48] Her courage proved exceptional as well. When she was thirty-three years old, Moon headed for China, where her sister was a missionary. Lottie led hundreds to the Lord and inspired Southern Baptist women back home to serve the missions cause. As she expended herself for the Chinese racked by war and disease, Moon withered away, weighing only fifty pounds before she died in 1912. The devotion to Christ that started with a revival in Charlottesville had reached the world and transformed a whole denomination. Still today, the annual Christmas offering named in her honor brings in the biggest portion of Southern Baptist money for missions.

Unity Ahead of Controversy

The revival of 1857 and 1858 also produced more immediate changes. Reports poured in from around the country indicating the revival's advance and effects.

The penitent owners of gambling saloons made them available for daily prayer meetings; southern grocery keepers rolled out their barrels, poured their contents on the ground, and "abandoned the traffic in ardent spirits"; the chief of police in Atlanta, Georgia, maintained that the revival had so reduced the rate of crime that he could dispense with half his force; in the fourth ward of New York City many "haunts of sin and shame" were shut up and "hundreds" of prostitutes allegedly "rescued."[49]

Several pastors sought to direct the revival fervor toward opposition to slavery. Plymouth Church in Brooklyn, led by Lyman Beecher's son Henry Ward, hosted prayer meetings starting on December 3, 1857. Like George Cheever at Congregational Church of the Puritans in New York, Beecher linked the revival with social activism, preaching against corporate sins such as slavery. Historian Timothy L. Smith observed how the revival fueled the engines of moral reform. "By the time of the Civil War the conviction had become commonplace that society must be reconstructed through the power of a sanctifying gospel and all the evils of cruelty, slavery, poverty, and greed be done away."[50]

On the other hand, Kathryn Long points to how the prayer meetings focused on individual conversion and barred anyone from addressing the hotly contested social debates of the day.[51] She sees few direct social effects of the revival. Rather, she argues that the revival offered sanctuary from the disputes that would soon plunge the United States into a civil war of unimaginable scale. "The 1857–58 Revival instead marked a transformation in Protestant attitudes toward conversionist piety and away from specific moral reforms," she writes.[52]

When considering the scope of the revival in 1857 and 1858, we may lament the startling absence of thoughtful Christian reflection on the looming war that escalated beyond any expectation.[53] But we should remember that the Christians who participated in the revival saw conversion as the key to reform and the greatest hope they could offer society. They carried this burden into the war with groups such as the United States Christian Commission, through which Moody and thousands more sought to relieve the spiritual and physical needs of soldiers. Some historians estimate that 2 million soldiers confessed Christ during revivals in military camps both North and South.

The revival also resulted in huge numbers of converts overseas. The 2,000 delegates who attended the Presbyterian Synod of Ireland during the 1858 general assembly in Dublin spent two sessions discussing revival in light of the events in the United States. The synod sent two pastors, including William Gibson, to visit the Fulton Street meetings.[54] Gibson would later compile reports from a revival that hit Northern Ireland in 1859 and resulted in 100,000 converts.[55]

The 1857–58 awakening testifies that God is not intimidated by the size of our cities and the sin found therein. His Holy Spirit can move through these cities again. God is looking for people like Jeremiah Lanphier who ask this question: "Lord, what would you have me to do?" He is looking for people of prayer. And he uses this prayer to bring the Christian unity that so often precedes and accompanies revival.

J. Edwin Orr wrote:

> The Great Awakening of 1857–58 produced the highest degree of real cooperation and unity among the various evangelical Christian denominations until then known in modern times. The general "zeal for souls" blurred denominational lines and diminished the denominational ambitions for aggrandizement. Some previous awakenings had been divisive in effect but this one witnesses the denominational walls "crumble to the earth before the heaven-descended impulse." The simple word "union" became the dominant description of the hundreds of prayer gatherings.[56]

NOTES

1. Kathryn Teresa Long, *The Revival of 1857–58: Interpreting an American Religious Awakening* (New York: Oxford University Press, 1998), 3.

2. Ibid., 7.

3. Ibid., 48.

4. J. Edwin Orr, *The Event of the Century: The 1857–1858 Awakening*, ed. Richard Owen Roberts (Wheaton, Ill.: International Awakening Press, 1989), 77.

5. Heman Humphrey, *Revival Sketches and Manual* (New York: American Tract Society, 1859), 277–78.

6. Long, *Revival of 1857–58*, 52.

7. "The Time for Prayer: The Third Great Awakening," *Christian History* 8 (Summer 1989): 32–33.

8. Cited in Orr, *Event of the Century*, 70.

9. Long, *Revival of 1857–58*, 103.

10. Orr, *Event of the Century*, 282.

11. Samuel Irenaeus Prime, *The Power of Prayer, Illustrated in the Wonderful Displays of Divine Grace at the Fulton Street and Other Meetings in New York and Elsewhere, 1857 and 1858* (New York: Charles Scribner, 1859), 20.

12. Ibid., 56.

13. Cited in Iain H. Murray, *Revival and Revivalism: The Making and Marring of American Evangelicalism 1750–1858* (Carlisle, Pa.: Banner of Truth Trust, 1994), 344.

14. "Time for Prayer," 32–33.

15. Richard Carwardine, *Transatlantic Revivalism: Popular Evangelicalism in Britain and America, 1790–1865* (Westport, Conn.: Greenwood Press, 1978), 27.

16. Orr, *Event of the Century*, 197.

17. *Ohio State Journal*, March 27, 1858, cited in Orr, *The Event of the Century*, 288.

18. Orr, *Event of the Century*, 86.

19. Ibid., 21.

20. Young Men's Christian Association (YMCA), *Pentecost or The Work of God in Philadelphia* (Philadelphia: Parry & McMillan, 1859).

21. Ibid., 1.

22. Ibid., 8.

23. Ibid., 9.

24. Ibid., 11–12.

25. Kenneth W. Osbeck, *Amazing Grace: 366 Inspiring Hymn Stories for Daily Devotions* (Grand Rapids: Kregel, 1990), 310.

26. YMCA, *Pentecost*, 67.

27. Ibid., 77–78.

28. Orr, *Event of the Century*, 121.

29. Ibid., 125.

30. "Time for Prayer," 32–33.

31. Orr, *Event of the Century*, 141.

32. *Appleton Post-Crescent*, April 10, 1858.

33. Orr, *Event of the Century*, 134.

34. Carwardine, *Transatlantic Revivalism*, 160.

35. "Time for Prayer," 32–33.

36. *Chicago Daily Press*, March 25, 1858.

37. *Chicago Daily Democrat*, April 20, 1858.

38. Orr, *Event of the Century*, 331.

39. Ibid., 188.

40. Ruth Bordin, *Frances Willard* (Chapel Hill: University of North Carolina Press, 1986), 28.

41. A. James Fuller, "The Way to Learn to Preach Is to Preach," in *John A. Broadus: A Living Legacy*, ed. David S. Dockery and Roger D. Duke (Nashville: B&H Academic, 2008), 58.

42. Ibid., 59.

43. Archibald Thomas Robertson, *Life and Letters of John Albert Broadus* (Philadelphia: American Baptist Publication Society, 1891), 104.

44. Ibid., 131.

45. Philip Alexander Bruce, *History of the University of Virginia, 1819–1919* (New York: Macmillan, 1921), 141–42.

46. Robertson, *Life and Letters of John Albert Broadus*, 145–46.

47. Catherine B. Allen, *The New Lottie Moon Story* (Nashville: Broadman, 1980), 35.

48. Ibid., 39.

49. Carwardine, *Transatlantic Revivalism*, 168.

50. Timothy L. Smith, *Revivalism and Social Reform: American Protestantism on the Eve of the Civil War* (Nashville: Abingdon, 1957), 161.

51. Long, *Revival of 1857–58*, 94.

52. Ibid., 126.

53. Harry S. Stout, *Upon the Altar to the Nation: A Moral History of the Civil War* (New York: Viking, 2006).

54. Wesley Duewel, *Revival Fire* (Grand Rapids: Zondervan, 1995), 137.

55. William Gibson, *The Year of Grace: A History of the Ulster Revival of 1859* (Edinburgh and London: Oliphant, Anderson & Ferrier, 1909), 17.

56. Orr, *Event of the Century*, 276.

- - - - - - - - - - - - - - - - - - - -

CHAPTER 5

DAWN OF THE CHRISTIAN CENTURY

Global Awakening, 1910s
WALES, INDIA, KOREA, NORTH AMERICA

No other nation can match Wales for frequency and fervency of revivals. Between 1760 and 1860, at least fifteen major revivals touched Wales, according to proud Welshman Martyn Lloyd-Jones.[1] Rare is the revival that has not passed through this little corner of the British Isles. These revivals have shaped Welsh identity. "Wales has to thank her past revivals for the greater part of the energy exhibited in her national, political and social life," a Baptist minister observed.

> In the revivals with which the people of Wales have been blessed of God, his Spirit engraved upon the conscience of the nation the terribly solemn truths of existence and the things which belong unto her peace. This gave to her men of conviction and of courage, and taught her to aspire to all that is good and noble, and whatever her achievements are religiously and socially, they are due mainly to the stimulus received during periods of outpouring of the Spirit of God.[2]

The Welsh have received revivals spreading from other countries as well as they have given them. Wales shared in the prayer meeting revivals that blessed the United States and Northern Ireland between 1857 and 1859. Methodist preacher Humphrey Jones, only twenty-seven years old, packed a chapel every morning at 5:00 a.m.

for five weeks at Tre'r-ddol in Wales. During evenings he led the meetings in prayer. As he traveled the country, Jones inspired David Morgan, who would go on to lead a four-hour communion service filled with tears and boisterous hymns juxtaposed with moments of silent reflection and confession. All told, the membership rolls of the Calvinistic Methodist Church grew by 3,000 during this revival wave.[3] But like its U.S. cousin, this Welsh revival brought denominations together in earnest prayer. "I thank God I have lived to see the year 1859," a Christian magazine reporter wrote. "God in His grace, has done more within the past two weeks in this part of the country than had been accomplished for an age previously."[4]

This legacy formed a foundation upon which God built another, even greater revival, starting in 1904. Self-described children of the earlier revival, including editor W. T. Stead, recognized the new movement of the Spirit and sought to aid its spread. "For as the mysterious outpouring of the blessing forty-three years ago has been of permanent help and strength and comfort to my own life ever since that time, so will this revival in Wales change, transform, inspire and glorify the lives of multitudes who at present know nothing and care nothing for the things that make for their own peace and the welfare of their fellow men," Stead wrote in 1905.[5]

The Lord Bends Wales

The first stirring of the last great Welsh revival began in Cardiganshire. Cutting through prolonged silence in response to a pastor's appeal, a lone Welsh girl spoke up. "If no one else will," she said, "then I must say that I do love my Lord Jesus Christ with all my heart."[6] She offered a fitting start to a revival where God answered the prayers of one devoted man equipped with the only qualification he would need to lead the awakening. Evan Roberts also loved the Lord Jesus Christ with all his heart. As he did with Jesus' disciples, God works mightily through those who know nothing except a desire to follow him and do his will.

Roberts was only twelve years old when he followed in his father's steps and began working in the famous Welsh coal mines that fueled the British Navy. A pious youth, Roberts carried his Bible down into the mine and occupied his mind by reciting favorite verses. Then Roberts worked briefly as a blacksmith, but he continued to pray that God would use him to bring revival to Wales. Finally, Roberts heeded a call to preach in 1904 and attended the Newcastle Emlyn academy to prepare for more advanced training at Trevecca College. But he never made it to Trevecca. By this time, several independent prayer initiatives had already sprouted across Wales. Roberts experienced a powerful work of the Spirit in September 1904 during a meeting led by Calvinist Methodist preacher Seth Joshua, who closed with the plea, "Lord … bend us." The phrase stuck with Roberts. He asked God to shape him, and the Lord responded by filling Roberts with zeal to see the world aflame with revival, starting with Wales.

He returned home to Loughor, where he had grown up attending Moriah Church. Starting October 31, 1904, Roberts led meetings for young people in the Calvinist Methodist congregation. A Sunday night service at the end of the first week kept Roberts awake until 3:15 a.m. It was undoubtedly worth the trouble. "The people were sitting, and only closed their eyes. The prayer began with me," Roberts said.

> Then it went from seat to seat—boys and girls—young men and maidens. Some asking in silence, some aloud, some coldly, some with warmth, some formally, some in tears, some with difficulty, some adding to it, boys and girls, strong voices, then tender voices. Oh, wonderful! I never thought of such an effect. I felt the place beginning to be filled, and before the prayer had gone half way through the chapel, I could hear some brother weeping, sobbing, and saying, "Oh, dear! Dear! Well! Well!" "Oh, dear! Dear!" On went the prayer, the feeling becoming more intense; the place being filled more and more (with the Spirit's presence).[7]

Roberts repeated a prayer over and over: "Send the Holy Spirit now, for Jesus Christ's sake." God would do that very thing. Soon churches throughout south Wales wanted to catch a glimpse of the anointed Roberts whose appeals brought such emotional responses.

Before November, at least 600 were converted. Joshua continued preaching at Ebenezer Chapel in Aberdare, and the revival moved north where it gained steam by combining with several preexisting local revivals. Roberts captivated the crowds with his evident intimacy with the Holy Spirit and expectant hope to see 100,000 converts in Wales. In one gripping personal vision, Roberts saw hell's fires flaring in a great pit circled by high walls and one entrance door, with masses pressing toward the pit. He asked God to relent and keep the door closed for just one year. Roberts's prayers found favor with the Lord.

"God has set his hand upon the lad, beautiful in simplicity, ordained in his devotion, lacking all the qualities that we have looked for in preachers and prophets and leaders," said G. Campbell Morgan, pastor of Westminster Chapel in London. "He has put him in the forefront of this movement that the world may see that he does choose the things that are not to bring to naught the things that are, the weak things of the world to confound the things that are mighty; a man who lacks all the essential qualities which we say make for greatness, in order that through him in simplicity and power he may move to victory."[8]

Roberts called upon Christians to pray for Wales. He believed the church of Jesus Christ on its knees is invincible. Roberts exhorted audiences toward greater faith and spiritual power. He urged them to confess all known sins and reconcile immediately with anyone they had wronged. He spurred Christians to shed any lingering doubt that hindered their relationship with God. He called on them to obey the Holy Spirit without flinching. And he urged all believers to make public profession of their faith in Christ. His messages were not noted for their expert handling of God's Word, even if they were consistent with its message. In singing-crazed Wales — a "nation of singing birds"[9] — music occupied as much as three-fourths of the lengthy meetings.

"No one uses a hymn-book. No one gives out a hymn," Stead wrote.

The last person to control the meeting in any way is Mr. Evan Roberts. People pray and sing, give testimony, exhort as the Spirit moves them. As a study of the psychology of crowds, I have seen nothing like it. You feel that the thousand of fifteen hundred persons before you have become merged into one myriad-headed but single-souled personality.[10]

If anyone spoke for too long, the crowd simply broke into song once more, Morgan reported. Even so, he observed no disorder. "When these Welshmen sing, they sing the words like men who believe them. They abandon themselves to their singing. We sing as though we thought it would not be respectable to be heard by the man next to us. No choir, did I say? It was all choir."[11]

Eventually hundreds of meetings filled Wales with the sounds of prayer, exhortation, and confession. The revival in south Wales grabbed most of the headlines, but the unprompted awakening up north was no less moving. A twenty-year-old preacher named Evan Lloyd Jones taught with unusual authority. Four months of revival in Rhos resulted in 2,267 converts, including an entire gang of thirteen miscreants.[12] Wales talked of little but the revival. Prayer spontaneously overtook political rallies. Even football matches had to be postponed. Observers traveled from around the world to see the great Evan Roberts. But the Welsh seemed to these outsiders strangely unconcerned whether or not Roberts visited them. The revival spread without need for any central coordination or advertisement.

Roberts desperately needed rest after nearly working himself to death by speaking at least sixteen hours each day. He paused for three weeks in February 1905 before traveling to Liverpool in England, where 750 Welsh converted. By June the revival began to wane. But Roberts's vision had been realized. An estimated 100,000 confessed Christ. The Congregationalists added 26,500 members. Another 24,000 Welsh joined the Calvinist Methodist Church. About 4,000 opted for the Wesleyan Church. The remainder were split between the Anglicans and several Baptist groups.[13] The effect on Welsh society was undeniable. Output from the coal mines famously slowed because the horses wouldn't move. Miners converted in the revival no longer kicked or swore at the horses, so the horses didn't know what to do.[14] Judges closed their courtrooms with nothing to judge. Christians wielded the revival as apologetic against the growing number of skeptics who derided religion. Stead argued:

> The most thoroughgoing materialist who resolutely and forever rejects as inconceivable the existence of the soul in man, and to whom "the universe is but the infinite empty eye-socket of a dead God," could not fail to be impressed by the pathetic sincerity of these men; nor, if he were just, could he refuse to recognize that out of their faith in the creed which he has rejected they have drawn, and are drawing, a motive power that makes for righteousness, and not only for righteousness, but for the joy of living, that he would be powerless to give them.[15]

Overseas Attention

Within a short time, American newspapers nationwide scrambled to run accounts of the Welsh revival. In remote Montana, the *Anaconda Standard* republished a report from the Welsh *Merthyr Express*. It emphasized youth leadership and the role of music. But the Montana newspaper sought to do more than simply pique interest. Local Welshman and pastor R. E. Williams appended his own commentary with application for area residents.

> Thus the revival, which our fellow countrymen have been long expecting and continually praying for, has come and is sweeping across the principality. At last it has broken out in several places in North Wales with leaps and bounds, bringing cheer to hundreds of Christian churches, to thousands of homes and of sin-distressed souls. Fellow Christians in Butte, shall we look for a similar blessing? We have the same promises as they, the same God to approach and the same need.[16]

Even as the revival slowed, American newspapers trumpeted the sensational events. In early March, the *Washington Post* devoted eight columns to the headline "Fervor of Religious Revival Stirs Two Continents."[17] The newspaper identified "throbs of a great religious awakening" in Wales, London, and half a dozen cities in America. The *Post* confirmed 100,000 conversions in Wales and said police found no crime to investigate amid "an almost complete realization of the Golden Rule in all affairs of daily life." A series of eighty evangelistic meetings led by R. A. Torrey and singer Charles Alexander in Albert Hall, London, earned special mention. The YMCA international committee chairman reported doubled interest in Bible study during the previous two years.

At the same time, the report previewed how European and American churches would lose the ultimate purpose and power of revival amid the era's quest for moral improvement. The *Washington Post* exalted individual conscience, personal morality, and biblical criticism, while proclaiming that the earth could become heaven if people would only "realize God" and follow the Golden Rule. Even as the world began to see revival as never before, the West began to lose the point. The united longing for revival that characterized the late 1850s fell apart. Some Protestants looked for revival to usher in a new age of peace and harmony. Others grew fascinated with emotional displays and supernatural gifts. Still more grew pessimistic about the state of affairs and focused on evangelistic campaigns that would save as many as possible. While once the methods of revival were contended, now the very nature and purpose of revival were up for grabs. Few held out hope for a revival such as previously experienced.

From Coal Mines to Mountains of Prayer

Though the Welsh Revival faded, a global awakening was brewing. Cutting against the grain of an era marked by emerging nationalism, revival forged ties across hardening political borders. News of revival in Wales encouraged laity and missionaries alike to pray for an outpouring of the Holy Spirit upon their own lands. In 1905 revival spread across Scandinavia, visiting Norway, Denmark, and Sweden. Travelers to Korea and China bore the exciting news and saw God work among them as never before. Indian believers welcomed an awakening they had prayed for and labored to see for decades. Local revivals sprouted up in several American cities, including Atlanta, Binghamton, Pueblo, Denver, Colorado Springs, and Terra Haute. Large crowds flocked to Azusa Street in Los Angeles between 1906 and 1907 to experience unusual manifestations of the Holy Spirit. Pentecostal churches multiplied and flourished in both the United States and overseas.[18] While political turmoil and mass-scale death loomed over the horizon, the first decade of the twentieth century held great promise for advancing the gospel of Jesus Christ worldwide through revival.

Following decades of missionary efforts by both Roman Catholics and Protestants, Christianity began to take hold among a Korean minority near the end of the 1800s. Missionaries persisted in prayer and Bible teaching in the hope that God would visit the Koreans with a powerful revival, but such spectacular results were not immediately forthcoming. Like so many other missionaries, Dr. R. A. Hardie was discouraged. The Canadian medical missionary working in Kangwon Province met with six other peers in Wosnan for prayer and Bible study in 1903. It was a tradition for Korean churches to set aside one week every year for nothing but small-group devotionals, and Hardie needed encouragement.

"I had for years been yearning to see Koreans convicted of sin and led to a repentance and faith evidencing the fruits thereof, but up to that time I had not seen any connection with my own work, any examples of plain, unmistakable, and lasting conversion," Hardie remembered. "I had seen many led to an intellectual knowledge and acceptance of these things, but I knew of few who gave any adequate evidence of knowing them as an actual and living experience. And these few were for the most part the results of the labor of others."[19]

During these meetings, the Methodist missionaries were led by M. C. White, visiting from China. Hardie was responsible for talking about prayer, a difficult task for a missionary battling doubt. He read from Luke 11:13, where Jesus explains that his heavenly Father gives the Holy Spirit to everyone who asks for him. Profoundly affected by this promise, Hardie confessed his pride and explained how he was depending on his own efforts, not on the Holy Spirit.

His honesty impressed and inspired the fellow missionaries. Hardie shared the experience with his Korean congregation, and the example of confession spread to others. The Koreans testified to a fresh sense of the Holy Spirit and openly confessed their sins. Several made restitution with one another for past wrongs, and some even reached outside the community of faith to make up for what they had done. After hearing of this revival, missionaries in Pyongyang, Korea's capital, invited Hardie to visit them in 1904 and share his experience. In Pyongyang and other Korean cities, the pattern of confession and restitution was repeated.

The Koreans could hardly imagine in 1905 what the next half century would hold for them. That year Japan claimed Korea as a protectorate. In the previous decade, Japan's growing military had defeated both China and Russia, and Korea was in no position to protest the move.[20] Yet the revival movement continued. At Seoul in September 1906, missionary Howard Agnew Johnston shared about the revivals simultaneously gripping Wales and regions of India. The Koreans were further encouraged to expect that God would work in powerful ways to revive their whole land. Indeed, the revival intensified during the opening week of 1907. Meeting in Pyongyang on January 6, 1907, about 1,500 missionaries and indigenous leaders persevered through momentary discouragement to offer expectant prayers. At one point, Korean leader Graham Lee asked for prayer, and several people led out at the same time. He responded, "If you want to pray like that, all pray," so all 1,500 prayed out loud at the same time. Many wept over their sins as they realized their need for God's grace and forgiveness. Leaders who harbored silent jealousy confessed and reconciled.

"The effect was indescribable—not confusion, but a vast harmony of sound and spirit, a mingling together of souls moved by an irresistible impulse of prayer," Presbyterian missionary William Blair remembered.

> The prayer sounded to me like the falling of many waters, an ocean of prayer beating against God's throne. It was not many, but one, born of one Spirit, lifted to one Father above. Just as on the day of Pentecost, they were all together in one place, of one

accord praying, "and suddenly there came from heaven the sound as of the rushing of a mighty wind, and it filled all the house where they were sitting." God is not always in the whirlwind, neither does he always speak in a still small voice. He came to us in Pyongyang that night with the sound of weeping. As the prayer continued, a spirit of heaviness and sorrow for sin came down upon the audience. Over on one side, someone began to weep, and in a moment the whole audience was weeping.[21]

The outpouring continued unabated until 2:00 a.m. Not every missionary condoned the unexpected enthusiasm and public confession. But confession humanized the missionaries, showing Koreans that the Westerners struggled with their own temptations and doubts. The outpouring helped Koreans who had wanted to impress the missionaries humble themselves and share intimate details about their real lives. Missionaries may have been shocked by what they learned, but the young Korean church took a giant step forward in spiritual maturity.

When the meetings concluded and the men returned home, they took the revival with them. Other communities experienced the same movement of confession and repentance. This was no mere emotional outpouring. Revived Christians sought to make reparations with those they had wronged. "It hurt so to see them grieve," Blair wrote. "All through the city men were going from house to house, confessing to individuals they had injured, returning stolen property and money, not only to Christians but to heathen as well, till the whole city was stirred. A Chinese merchant was astonished to have a Christian walk in and pay him a large sum of money that he had obtained unjustly years before."[22]

Canadian missionary Jonathan Goforth was so thrilled by what he heard about the revival that he traveled from China to Korea in 1907 to see for himself. "I need hardly say how greatly I rejoiced at such an opportunity," Goforth remembered. "The Korean movement was of incalculable significance in my life because it showed me at first-hand the boundless possibilities of the revival method. It is one thing to read about Revival in books. To witness its working with one's own eyes and to feel its atmosphere with one's own heart is a different thing altogether. Korea made me feel, as it did many others, that this was God's plan for setting the world aflame."[23]

Scholars have offered several reasons for the Korean revival. Perhaps the repressive Japanese rule agitated Koreans and sent them looking for new spiritual sanctuaries. Or maybe as Korea opened to Western influence, they wanted to emulate Western religious rhythms. Or it could be that the Christian missionaries simply delivered a compelling alternative to shamanism, Confucianism, and Buddhism, even as they labored to explain the similarities without intimidating potential converts. Even taking into account these factors, it is hard to account fully for the sudden, remarkable growth of Korean churches. Between 1906 and 1907, the Presbyterian churches grew from 54,987 members to 73,844. The Methodists grew from 18,107 in 1906 to 39,613 in 1907.[24] Extending this range to a five-year period, Korean churches altogether added 80,000 converts, more than the total number of Christian converts during eighty years of missionary activity in neighboring China.[25]

As the revival translated into aggressive, effective evangelism, Korean churches began to grow independent of missionary support. The transition came just in time, because the Japanese brutally persecuted Koreans from 1910 until the end of World War II in 1945. Though Korea was conquered, the church grew stronger and built enduring structures.[26]

The revival also launched several distinct practices that have become closely associated with Korean Christians. Decades later, Wesley Duewel reported that one-third of Korean church members still arose for daily prayer meetings at 5:00 a.m.[27] Koreans still pray out loud simultaneously and evangelize courageously, sending more cross-cultural missionaries than any other nation except the United States.[28]

Those swept up in the revivals during the first decade of the twentieth century might not have anticipated exactly how the church would flourish. But they knew that God had started something powerful. During the 1908 General Assembly of the Methodist Episcopal Church, Bishop M. C. Harris offered an account of the revival.

The effects following this movement are wholly good — the church raised up to a higher spiritual level, almost entire absence of fanaticism because of previous careful instruction in the Bible; not one case of insanity, but many thousands clothed in their right mind; scores of men called to the holy ministry; greater congregations, searching the Word, as many as two thousand meeting in one place for the study of the Bible; many thousands learning to read, and making inquiries; multitudes of them pressing upon the tired missionary and native pastors praying, "Give us to eat." I beseech you do not listen to any word suggestions of doubt as to the vitality and reality of this. Drunkards, gamblers, thieves, adulterers, murderers, self-righteous Confucianists and dead Buddhists, and thousands of devil-worshipers have been made new men in Christ, the old things gone forever.[29]

The Korean awakening showed how revival can even touch nations without a dominant Christian culture. Many religious leaders had supposed that Christian nominalism was a necessary precursor to revival. Yet the Korean revival brought spectacular growth to a small Christian minority amid a culture hostile to their faith. Perhaps the outpouring should not have surprised anyone familiar with Jonah's mission to Nineveh. The prophet certainly did not expect Nineveh would heed the warning he reluctantly delivered. But heed it they did, turning from their sins in the faint hope that God might relent from destroying the city. Indeed, God spared the wicked Assyrian city, much to Jonah's dismay (Jonah 3 – 4). The episode might not fit classical definitions of revival, but it shares the characteristics of wide-scale confession and repentance.

The Power of a Praying Woman

Like Korea, India had been the target of long-term missionary efforts since the early 1900s. But by and large, the nation remained resolutely Hindu. This ancient religion dominated every sphere of life. From young ages, children born into the privileged castes carefully studied the Hindu scriptures. When Pandita Ramabai was only twelve years old, she had memorized 18,000 verses from the Hindu Puranas. Young Pandita excelled under the tutelage of her mother. Ramabai's father advocated for women's education against the wishes of most Hindu leaders. No one could doubt his religious devotion, however. He continued worshiping Hindu idols and hosting religious pilgrims to the point of depleting all his family's resources. Impoverished, Ramabai's mother, father, and sister were severely weakened by hunger and died when she was sixteen.

Ramabai vowed she would help society's vulnerable women, especially orphans and widows. She spoke publicly on their behalf before Calcutta's wise men, known as pandits, impressing them with learning practically unknown for an Indian woman. They called her Goddess of Wisdom, and Ramabai became the only woman called Pandita for her wisdom. "She was unimagined—a woman of purest Brahman birth, twenty years old and unmarried, beautiful and impossibly learned," Mary Lucia Bierce Fuller wrote. "She dazzled India."[30]

Ramabai married a Bengali man who, like her, had abandoned Hinduism for theism. But he died of cholera when their only child was not yet one year old. Already an orphan, Ramabai was now also a widow. Undaunted, she continued her quest to educate women, even wielding the Hindu scriptures she still knew so well against the Brahmans. To aid in her advocacy, Ramabai studied English in Poona with a Christian woman and was invited to visit England. Before departing, several friends warned her against converting. After she came ashore in 1883, the Church of England Sisterhood at Wantage hosted her. A visit to their rescue shelter for women made a big impression. She had never known Hindus to care for women in this way. "I had not heard anyone speaking kindly of them, nor seen anyone making any effort to turn them from the evil path they had chosen in their folly," Ramabai wrote. "The Hindu Shastras do not deal kindly with these women. The law of the Hindu commands that the kind shall cause the fallen women to be eaten by dogs in the outskirts of town. They are considered the greatest sinners, and not worthy of compassion."[31]

The Anglican sisters explained to Ramabai how Jesus treated the Samaritan woman he met at Jacob's well (John 4). After studying the Bible for herself, Ramabai was baptized, along with her little girl. But acknowledging the Christian religion did not yet imply that Ramabai had found Christ himself. She found him, though, when she studied the Bible more carefully and read passages such as Romans 5:6–10 and 1 John 4:9–10 that explained God's free grace imparted to those who believe without regard for their personal merits. "What good news for me, a woman, a woman born in India, among Brahmans who hold out no hope for me and the likes of me!" Ramabai exclaimed. "The Bible declares that Christ did not reserve this great salvation for a particular caste or sex."[32]

For the remainder of her trip to Britain, Ramabai taught Sanskrit at Cheltenham Ladies' College and dabbled in other subjects, including mathematics, literature, and science. Pleas from home induced her to return to India and start a school in Bombay for high-caste widows. She moved the school after a year to Poona, and resisted evangelizing except by making the Bible available alongside other religious texts. Still, she hoped and prayed for spiritual inquiries. Indeed, one woman converted to Christianity, prompting Brahmans to withdraw twenty-five other widows from the school. Undaunted, Ramabai continued to take up the women's cause when few others cared. She fought government opposition to her efforts to save hundreds of widows suffering during a great famine in 1896. She bought a hundred-acre farm in Kedagon, about thirty-four miles from Poona, a "treeless, shelterless, waterless place,"[33] where she hoped the community could support themselves without Western assistance. Here she offered protection for 1,350 women and children during the deadly Gujarat famine in 1900. She named the site Mukti, meaning "salvation." "Anywhere on those busy hundred acres might be seen the indomitable little generalissimo—in her spotless widow's white—who, like George Mueller, trusted God as if all depended on Him, and worked as if all depended on her," Fuller wrote.[34]

Ramabai's Christian convictions deepened and became more overt in Mukti. Already fluent in six Indian languages, she learned

Pandita Ramabai (second row from bottom, second from left) was especially encouraged by news of the Welsh revival. (Courtesy of the American Council of the Ramabai Mukti Mission.)

Greek and Hebrew to produce her own Marathi translation of the Bible. Western travel exposed her to teaching about revival, and when speaking in 1898 before the Keswick Convention in Britain, she asked Christians to pray for revival in India. Already, Mukti rejoiced over great salvation harvests in 1901 and 1902. Ramabai eagerly longed for news of global revival. Encouraged by Australia's warm reception of Torrey and Alexander in 1903, Ramabai dispatched Mukti girls to ask new Christians in Australia to pray for India. The Welsh revival in particular filled Ramabai with great hope. So she started a prayer circle in 1905. Every morning they gathered to pray for Indian Christians and global revival. The Mukti girls prayed in groups of ten. At first, about 250 girls met regularly. Eventually, 550 gathered twice each day to pray for revival. Within two months, they saw 1,200 conversions. After six months, Ramabai pronounced that God had revived Mukti. The new Christians were zealous in preaching the gospel wherever they traveled.[35]

Mukti wasn't the only revival that shook India. As soon as Ramabai heard about the Assam revival in northeast India, she asked for evangelism volunteers, and thirty girls stepped forward. When praying together to prepare for the task, the Spirit moved among the girls. "One of the thirty volunteers was so set aflame spiritually that the other girls saw a vision of fire engulfing and surrounding her," Wesley Duewel wrote. "One of the other girls ran across the room to grab a pail of water to throw on her, only to discover that the fire, though visible, was not literal. It was the fire of the Spirit as seen in Old Testament times and at Pentecost."[36]

The next day, June 30, 1905, the whole Mukti school was gripped so tightly by conviction of sin that they could not work until they were assured of forgiveness. Ramabai dispatched praying bands to Pune for evangelism and teaching. Throughout the awakening, coordinated evangelism, prayer, and relief teams from Mukti stoked the revival fires. The revival continued through the next year and touched several Indian regions. Speaking at Dohnavour in October 1906, missionary Amy Carmichael suddenly needed to stop because she felt overwhelmed by God's presence. "It was so startling and so awful," Carmichael remembered. "I can use no other word, the details escape me. Soon the whole upper half of the church was on its face on the floor crying to God, each boy and girl, man and woman, oblivious of all others. The sound was like the sound of waves or strong wind in the trees. No separate voice could be heard."[37] In other corners of India, Welsh missionaries told of their native revival, prompting similar outpourings of teary confessions and pleas for forgiveness. Two countries, unlike one another in so many ways, shared the common bond of a revival that confounded skeptics and built the church.

Gone as Quickly as It Came

At the dawn of the Christian century, it must have looked as if the whole world might soon enter the kingdom of God. The missionary efforts launched during previous awakenings gained momentum as the mere mention of revival seemed enough to cut through tough terrain in places like Korea and India. More than a hundred years later, we may celebrate Korea's transformation and rejoice in the sturdy Indian churches that continue to proclaim the gospel despite withering persecution. But we also know that Wales seems to have entirely forgotten its revival legacy. Wales is perhaps more immune to revival today because it has been inoculated with heavy doses of undiluted religious fervor.

In retrospect, we can see warning signs embedded in the last great Welsh revival. Evan Roberts faded from the scene in late 1905 and needed a prolonged retreat in 1906. Ecstasy aside, his shortcomings became apparent. Roberts, a gifted exhorter who led meetings filled with prayers, singing, and testimonies, did not prioritize Bible teaching. Compared to the 1859 revival, fewer Welsh preachers taught biblical doctrine. Instead, many new converts sought mystical experiences.[38] Without basic biblical formation, many caught up in the revival lacked the necessary tools for spiritual growth.

"This gave rise to some excesses of emotionalism, and placed the converts' experience at the mercy of individual idiosyncrasies and the psychological fashions of the day," Eifon Evans wrote. "The later repercussions were even more serious, for it led to a rapid decline in the spiritual discernment and vigour of many, whose love, unbuttressed by knowledge, grew sadly cold."[39]

Until his death, Roberts continued to intercede in prayer for his native land. But he damaged his and the revival's reputation with scandalous behavior. His negative example soured many on the merits of revival.[40] Why bother if we have so little to show for all the fuss? A closer examination, however, reveals long-term significant contributions. Six years after the Welsh revival, 80 percent of converts were still members of the church they joined during the awakening. Many of the remaining 20 percent had simply joined a different body.[41] If Christianity declined rapidly in Wales as Europe descended into world war, imagine what might have happened without the revival. "Throughout the lean years of declension in the churches which followed the 1914–18 war it was the 'children of the revival' who maintained the spiritual glow in the prayer and society meeting and Sunday School," Evans wrote. "The faithful remnant within each denomination consisted mainly of the rank and file of revival converts."

Even so, the effects of revival are admittedly difficult to quantify. But do we ask too much of revival by demanding verifiable, documented results of all that took place? Gomer Roberts asked rhetorically:

> Who can give an account of the lasting blessings of the 1904–5 revival? Is it possible to tabulate a sum total of family bliss, peace of conscience, brotherly love, and holy conversation? What of the debts that were paid, and the enemies reconciled to one another? What of the drunkards who became sober, and the prodigals who were restored? Is there a balance that can weigh the burden of sins which were throw at the foot of the cross?[42]

After several years, Wales returned to its previous state of religious indifference. Many converts persevered, but revival enthusiasm departed as quickly as it appeared. But in the eyes of Martyn Lloyd-Jones, the fleeting nature of revival merely proves that a sovereign God "giveth and taketh away." We cannot bind him to send revival, and we cannot prevent him from withdrawing. Who can know his ultimate purposes? Even if the Christian century didn't unfold as hoped in Wales, we can still celebrate a precious time when God seemed to offer earth a fresh taste of heaven's bliss.

"It is, of course, best of all when a consecrated life is crowned by a triumphant death. But it is not a bad thing—on the contrary, it is a very good thing—to raise human lives to a higher moral level for a comparatively short period, even if after that time they all slide back," Stead wrote. "It is better to have lived well for a year than never to have been above the mire at all."[43]

NOTES

1. D. M. Lloyd-Jones, "Revival: An Historical and Theological Survey," in *The Puritans: Their Origins and Successors; Addresses Delivered at the Puritan and Westminster Conferences 1959–1978* (Carlisle, Pa.: Banner of Truth Trust, 1987), 4.

2. Cited in W. T. Stead, "A Narrative of Facts," in *The Welsh Revival* (Boston: Pilgrim Press, 1905), 13–14.

3. Wesley Duewel, *Revival Fire* (Grand Rapids: Zondervan, 1995), 163.

4. Thomas Phillips, *The Welsh Revival* (Edinburgh: Banner of Truth Trust, 1989), 9–10.

5. Stead, "Narrative of Facts," 13–14.

6. Ibid., 42–43.

7. Duewel, *Revival Fire*, 190.

8. G. Campbell Morgan, "The Revival: Its Power and Source," in *The Welsh Revival* (Boston: Pilgrim Press, 1905), 82.

9. Stead, "Narrative of Facts," 29.

10. Ibid., 45.

11. Morgan, "The Revival: Its Power and Source," 82.

12. Duewel, *Revival Fire*, 199.

13. Earle E. Cairns, *An Endless Line of Splendor: Revivals and Their Leaders from the Great Awakening to the Present* (Wheaton, Ill.: Tyndale, 1986), 196.

14. Stead, "Narrative of Facts," 41–42.

15. Ibid., 41.

16. *Anaconda Standard*, Friday morning, December 30, 1904, 10.

17. *Washington Post*, March 12, 1905, 4.

18. Grant Wacker, *Heaven Below: Early Pentecostals and American Culture* (Cambridge, Mass.: Harvard University Press, 2001).

19. Donald D. Owens, *Revival Fires in Korea* (Kansas City, Mo.: Nazarene Publishing House, 1977), 26.

20. Mark Shaw, *Global Awakening: How 20th-Century Revivals Triggered a Christian Revolution* (Downers Grove, Ill.: InterVarsity, 2010), 35.

21. William Blair and Bruce Hunt, *The Korean Pentecost and the Sufferings Which Followed* (Carlisle, Pa.: Banner of Truth Trust, 1977), 71–72.

22. Ibid., 75.

23. Jonathan Goforth, *"By My Spirit"* (London: Marshall, Morgan & Scott, 1929), 28.

24. Young-Hoon Lee, "Korean Pentecost: The Great Revival of 1907," in *Asian Journal of Pentecostal Studies* 4, no.1 (2001): 81.

25. Duewel, *Revival Fire*, 257–58.

26. Lee, "Korean Pentecost," 81.

27. Duewel, *Revival Fire*, 257.

28. Rob Moll, "Missions Incredible," *Christianity Today*, March 2006, 28–34.

29. Joseph B. Hingeley, ed., *Journal of the Twenty-fifth Delegated General Conference of the Methodist Episcopal Church, Baltimore, MD, May 6–June 1, 1908* (New York: Eaton & Mains, 1908), 861–62.

30. Mary Lucia Bierce Fuller, *The Triumph of an Indian Widow* (Philadelphia: American Council of the Ramabai Mukti Mission, 1939), 17.

31. Pandita Ramabai, *A Testimony* (Kedgaon, Poona: Ramabai Mukti Mission, 1968), 19–20.

32. Ibid., 26.

33. Fuller, *Triumph of an Indian Widow*, 45–46.

34. Ibid., 54.

35. Ramabai, *Testimony*, 36.

36. Duewel, *Revival Fire*, 217.

37. Ibid., 230.

38. Cairns, *Endless Line of Splendor*, 196–97.

39. Eifion Evans, *The Welsh Revival of 1904* (Bridgend: Evangelical Press of Wales, 1969), 163–64.

40. Iain H. Murray, *Pentecost — Today? The Biblical Basis for Understanding Revival* (Carlisle, Pa.: Banner of Truth Trust, 1998), 159–61.

41. Duewel, *Revival Fire*, 202.

42. Evans, *Welsh Revival of 1904*, 162.

43. Stead, "Narrative of Facts," 36–37.

CHAPTER 6

INDIGENOUS INSPIRATION

East Africa Revival, 1920s to 1970s
EAST AFRICA

The Western-focused perspective on world history looks at the first half of the twentieth century and sees significant Christian decline and loss. European churches, weakened by internal disputes and rocked by revolutions, could not stop the outbreak of two wars that claimed millions of dead around the world. Likewise, American churches split into camps of modernists and fundamentalists, weakening the nation's long-standing Protestant establishment. Yet from the global perspective, Christianity thrived as never before between 1900 and the end of World War II. In particular the revival that broke out in east-central Africa in 1930 reshaped the continent's religious makeup. For nearly half a century, revivals big and small bolstered the African church, especially in Burundi, Rwanda, and Uganda. The so-called East African Revival nursed the health of a growing church that would survive severe persecution and genocide during the latter half of the bloody twentieth century. Observers of the awakening insist the world has never seen anything like it. Decades later, nearly all of East Africa's Protestant church leaders had been shaped by the revival.

Kindred Spirits

Though divided between liberal and conservative factions, the Church Missionary Society launched a mission in Rwanda in 1920. This Church of England missionary venture grew quickly but without adequate depth. New converts could not shake their sin, and leaders succumbed to moral corruption. The church had established a beachhead in tough terrain, but like much of the West, nominalism hindered church vitality and growth.

Dr. Joe Church, backed by the Cambridge Inter-Collegiate Christian Union (CICCU), left behind the promise of a prestigious career back home to pursue his missionary calling. Educated in the best English schools, cultured in proper English ways, Church arrived in Gahini, Rwanda, in 1928 and threw himself into medical missionary work. But within the first year, the man was overwhelmed by the region's physical and spiritual needs. About 250,000 Africans living around Gahini had no prior access to medicine or the gospel. His hospital was a collection of huts fashioned from grass. He and other missionaries used them to distribute food to the famine-starved masses. Some days, 1,000 refugees fleeing famine passed through Gahini.

"The shacks were packed with thin apathetic people sitting over the embers of their fires, just waiting, many of them lying about ill with fever and exhaustion and covered with the disease of yaws and flies," Church remembered. "They held their hands out begging as we passed and some of the naked children tried to run after us a little way."[1]

What Church witnessed day after day would be enough to bring the strongest man to tears. Just before going to sleep one night, Church and fellow missionary Bert Jackson heard what they thought to be a jackal in the garden. "With a torch and shotgun we searched," Church wrote. "The strange noise went on from time to time and then stopped, so, after finding nothing we went to bed. The next morning I found a completely naked starving man who had crawled as far as the garden and died." Around this same time, Jackson asked Church to help him check on a stench emanating from something in his bathtub. "We pulled aside a sheet and found a living skeleton of a boy, just alive, who had crawled into the bathroom and pulled a sheet over him and gone to sleep," Church said. "He was covered from head to foot in sores."[2]

The signs of physical decay were a stiff reminder of the region's great spiritual need. But Church couldn't always count on help from his fellow missionaries. He angered the hospital staff by insisting that they travel through the villages preaching the gospel. Colleagues protested that they should be exempt from this work as medical missionaries. Church could not even turn to his fiancée, for she remained home in England, too ill with arthritis and measles to join him in the unforgiving African mission field.

"I think in many ways this is one of the heaviest and blackest moments in my life," Church wrote home to his fiancée. "The Lord is as real as ever, but I just cannot see an inch ahead. I often feel that my witness for Christ must be almost nix. I am just trying all the more to give the Lord absolutely everything, and then to praise Him, and wait for His guiding hand."

Church began to see more clearly when he traveled to Namirembe Hill in Kampala, Uganda, on Saturday, September 22, 1929. Kampala, "set amid the beauty of flowering trees, yellow cassias, scarlet flame trees, and blue jacarandas,"[3] sat below the Anglican cathedral with a dome that beckoned the masses for miles. That day Church met a kindred spirit, Simeon Nsibambi. Dressed in the type of dark suit worn by prosperous British businessmen, Nsibambi approached Church as he walked to the Anglican service. They had met earlier that year when Church taught a Bible class. Nsibambi, Uganda's chief health officer, had been born into Uganda's Anglican mission in 1897. His father, a Christian tribal chief, had him baptized at the cathedral on Namirembe Hill and sent him to schools in Kampala run by the Church Missionary Society. Living comfortably near the cathedral, Nsibambi and his wife, Eva, aided the poor through the Good Samaritan Society. Though not a gifted public speaker, he enjoyed singing with the cathedral choir.[4] Yet he longed for a more powerful, intimate experience with God. Nsibambi wanted to know if Church had anything else to teach him.

"I said that I was looking for a new infilling of the Holy Spirit and the victorious life," said Church, an ardent proponent of Keswick theology. Keswick refers to conventions in England that encourage pursuit of a higher Christian life of holiness. "He warmed to this as we talked. I had been praying for a long time that God would lead me to one really saved African with whom I could have deep fellowship. God was answering that prayer that Sunday morning, when something happened that changed the course of my missionary career."[5]

Meeting with Church, Nsibambi brought along a friend who shared his desire to learn more about the Spirit-filled life. After studying C. I. Scofield's study notes on the Holy Spirit, the three men knelt to renounce their sin and claim the "victorious life." Church excitedly wrote home to his prayer partners in Cambridge. "There could be a Revival in the Uganda Church if there was someone who could come, Spirit-filled, and point these thousands of nominal Christians to the Victorious Life," Church said. "Pray for this—a real deepening of Spiritual life and conviction of sin in the Uganda Church, and then the out-pouring of the Spirit Himself will follow."

It may be hard to imagine that the young church in Uganda could already need revival little more than fifty years after missionaries arrived, when only about one-third of Ugandans professed Christ. But the mission had grown rapidly in just a few decades. By 1893 Uganda had already commissioned 260 evangelists. The entire Bible had been translated and widely distributed before 1910. Churches welcomed believers across tribal boundaries. Ugandans embraced the gospel more quickly and enthusiastically than any other Africans during this initial missionary thrust. They wielded a "disproportionate share of social, economic, and political power and dominated government. All the members of the governing council (*lukiko*) and nearly all the chiefs were Christians."[6]

But this power and prosperity created a big problem. Namely, Uganda's established churches had a lot in common with their Western counterparts. Nominalism infected the church nearly as quickly as God had gathered it. Missionaries such as Mabel Ensor with the Church Missionary Society had pleaded with Ugandans to return to God and forsake the native rituals they had resumed. Frustrated by not seeing signs of revival, Ensor eventually quit the Church Missionary Society in 1928. Other missionaries, including Church, persevered and began to see change in 1929. Wherever the Lord would take him from his encounter with Nsibambi, Church would never forget this answer to prayer. When he reached the end of himself, Church found the risen Jesus Christ.

Church later learned how the meeting had changed Nsibambi too. As he headed home to Rwanda, Church bumped into a missionary who asked him, "What did you do to Nsibambi?" Church responded, "Why, what's the matter?" The woman told him, "Oh, he's gone mad and is going round everywhere asking people if they are saved. He's just left my gardener." She did not believe it was appropriate for Africans to teach about the Holy Spirit and sanctification.[7] Even so, Nsibambi couldn't help but testify to the power of God. He ditched his European suits and designer shoes in favor of a flowing white robe and bare feet. He resigned his plum government job and sold off many of his belongings. He began to preach around

British medical missionary Joe Church (middle row, white suit) was invigorated by meeting Africans on his staff at Gahini Hospital and elsewhere who shared his longing for revival. (Courtesy of the Joe Church Collection, Henry Martyn Centre, Gahini University of Cambridge.)

Kampala. He led preaching teams that sought audiences for the gospel wherever they encountered a crowd. Measured and sociable, Nsibambi thrived while meeting individually with inquirers who wanted to know the secret of his fervor and joy.

Back in Rwanda, Church was invigorated. A New Testament translation was published in 1931. Unlike earlier African awakenings, this revival created substantial unity. Danish Baptists, American Friends, Anglicans, Free Methodists, and Nazarenes joined together in the Protestant Alliance of Rwanda-Burundi in 1935. Turnover on the Gahini hospital staff changed the whole mission's tone. Unlike those who rebuffed Church's pleas for evangelism when he arrived, these new staff members somehow surpassed him in zeal. He recommended the staff meet at 5:00 a.m. for prayer. They politely informed him that they were already meeting two hours before sunrise to pray.

Indeed, God answered their prayers for spiritual blessing. Jim Brazier, later a bishop, returned from vacation to learn that revival had spread through small churches around Kigeme, Rwanda. "I arrived back to find Revival in over twenty villages with the same accompaniments as we had on the station, conviction and confession of sin under great emotional stress, followed by great joy and zeal to win others," Brazier wrote on December 12, 1936. "It was a common practice for the whole congregation to spend the whole night in the village church, chiefly in prayer and praise. A feature of this conviction was that it came as a result of prayer and not as a result of preaching. These 'revived' people are a joy to question for Baptism. Whereas it is often hard work to draw anything spontaneous from the average candidate, these are just full of what the Lord has done for them."[8]

The revival started small with bands that fanned out and preached to their neighbors before taking the gospel message to nearby towns. The converts would then congregate in small groups to hold each other accountable to the commitments they made. These accountability groups recalled the eighteenth-century Evangelical Awakening, when British Methodists covenanted together in regular class meetings. Finally, as entire regions and nations in

Africa experienced revival, the leaders organized conventions that sustained the movement's focus on holiness, reconciliation, and evangelism. Wherever the *Abaka* ("those on fire" or "those who glow") gathered, they sang the revival anthem "Tukutendereza Yesu" ("We Praise You, Jesus").

Precious Saviour, Thou hast saved me;
    Thine, and only Thine, I am;
Oh, the cleansing blood has reached me!
    Glory, glory to the Lamb!

Glory, glory, hallelujah!
    Glory, glory to the Lamb!
Oh, the cleansing blood has reached me!
    Glory, glory to the Lamb!

Long my yearning heart was striving
    To obtain this precious rest;
But, when all my struggles ended,
    Simply trusting I was blessed.

Trusting, trusting every moment;
    Feeling now the blood applied,
Lying in the cleansing fountain,
    Dwelling in my Saviour's side.

Consecrated to Thy service,
    I will live and die to Thee;
I will witness to Thy glory,
    Of salvation, full and free.

Yes, I will stand up for Jesus,
    He has sweetly saved my soul,
Cleansed my soul from sin's corruption,
    Sanctified, and made me whole.

Glory to the Lord who bought me,
    Glory for His saving power;
Glory to the Lord who keeps me,
    Glory, glory evermore!

The hymn captures how East Africans expected revival to continue for the rest of their Christian lives. Church wrote, "Revival for them is the blessing of the gospel *continuously*; the same grace that meets the sinner when he first comes to Christ is ministered to his heart unceasingly all through his Christian life."[9] Church believed God is not "capricious" to send revival only when he pleases. Christians never need to wait for revival, Church taught, because Jesus never comes and goes. He is constant. And he blesses Christians who pray with conviction, repent of their sins, pursue the fullness and power of the Holy Spirit, open themselves to accountability, and seek unity. Influenced by these marks of Keswick theology, the Anglicans managed to largely avoid the fixation on signs and wonders that characterized the revival among independent African churches. Instead, they pursued reconciliation with God, one another, and their other neighbors. God demonstrated his power by healing some sick, but "saved ones" more commonly pointed to the healing balm of salvation from Jesus Christ, who gave his life on the Cross for sin.[10]

Africans Dig Deeper

As indigenous leaders shouldered more of the revival's responsibility, the movement dug deeper into African soil. Seeds planted by Church and Nsibambi grew up and bore fruit. William Nagenda had arrived at Gahini in 1937 after he was converted under Nsibambi's ministry. Like Nsibambi, he was highly educated and a polished English speaker. Yet he longed for chances to give his life in missionary service.

"The need of so many all over Uganda and my inability to help them has forced and constrained me to take a new step in faith and to ask God to fill me with the Holy Spirit of power," Nagenda explained to Church in 1942. "I know He has done it; the manifestations of the Holy Spirit, I have no doubt, will be seen in my life in His time. We can't go on like this; the world is perishing and I hear His voice calling me to take responsibility not only for Uganda, but for Africa, and the whole world."[11]

By this time, the whole world was subsumed by war. In the aftermath, tensions mounted between Western missionaries and Africans partial to nationalistic movements. But the revival demonstrated its ongoing power by humbling Christians on both sides to preserve the bonds of fellowship. Church believed that unity between white missionaries and Africans was the revival's greatest outcome. He and his team were prepared for the challenge because they had already aired and addressed the racial tension. He wrote in 1933, "We found that when once we had repented and in some cases asked forgiveness for our prejudice and white superiority, a new realm of relationships was entered into which altered the character of all our work."[12]

Nevertheless, Church expressed excessive enthusiasm when he wrote, "Revival answers every problem."[13] In fact, the revival raised a whole new set of problems. As was alleged of Wesley's Methodists, confession looked to some like spiritual one-upmanship. They feared that the revived Christians looked down on them as spiritual inferiors. As with rigorous early church movements that weathered Roman persecution, such as the Montanists and Donatists, many church officials viewed the East African Revival as a schismatic threat. The Roman Catholic Church, which arrived in Rwanda twenty-seven years before the Anglicans, obstructed the Protestants where they could in these days before the reforms of Vatican II. Even Church eventually admitted that revival almost always leads to controversy and division.[14]

The problem was most acute in Uganda. Reminiscent of the First Great Awakening in the United States, revived Africans studying for the ministry at Bishop Tucker Theological College in Mukono challenged their teachers, most of whom did not support the revival. The students believed teachers had compromised with modern theology and no longer held to the doctrines of original sin and Jesus' substitutionary atonement on the Cross. They also clashed over the need for believers to separate from society and even other Christians at times to pursue holiness. The school quelled the challenge by expelling twenty-six students, including Nagenda.

Facing mounting opposition, Bishop C. E. Stuart clamped down on criticism of church leaders and discouraged public confession of sin. Try as he might, he could not maintain unity between factions loyal to the Student Christian Movement, which favored the social gospel, and CICCU, which emphasized personal conversion. Stuart rejected Church's appeals to start a convention for Christians seeking the higher life. When Church explored alternatives, Stuart believed he was undermining ecclesial authority. Stuart suspended Church from preaching in Uganda and withdrew his lay reader's license. He ordered every church to announce and enforce the ban.

Trouble Brews in Kenya

Meanwhile, trouble was brewing in another nation touched by the revival. By 1957, Protestant church membership in Kenya had grown dramatically to 291,118.[15] But interracial tension threatened to tear apart the nation and the revival. Hoping to profit from the rich African soil and abundant indigenous labor, the British Empire had colonized Kenya in 1920. In the process, British settlers confiscated tribal lands they believed no one occupied. Poor wages paid to native Kenyans didn't help matters either. Rebellion began to brew.[16]

As Kenyans who fought in World War II returned home, their resentment toward the white settlers boiled over, particularly among the Kikuyu tribe. Leaders schemed to kill Europeans and incite a national revolution. They also aimed to expel the religion these whites brought with them. Some Kikuyu resented missionary criticism of traditional practices such as female circumcision. "Jesus didn't live here before the British came," derisive Kikuyu argued. "He came on the first boat that brought these white people to our land. When the white rulers go home, they can take their Jesus with them!"[17] Most Kikuyu pledged allegiance to the revolution, a commitment that included denouncing the Christian faith that many of them practiced nominally. In 1952 war erupted between these forces, called the Mau Mau, and the British military.

J. Edwin Orr visited Kenya in 1953, when two thousand Kenyan believers, called "saved ones," braved a Mau Mau stronghold in Nairobi for a convention celebrating God's work in the revival. "The speaker was a Kikuyu clergyman, face scarred, partly paralysed from a slashing received for refusing to deny Christ," Orr remembered. "His was a message of freedom, freedom from hatred of other tribes and races, freedom from fear. It was the same in a little gathering on the edge of the Aberdare Forest, addressed by the writer, the meeting concluded with singing 'Tukutendereza Yesu.'" Orr noted two reasons revival advocates faced persecution. First, they preached the gospel of Jesus Christ with boldness. Second, revival reconciled whites and blacks and restored trust between tribes.[18]

Great Britain finally gave Kenya its independence at the end of 1963, but not before British armed forces spent seven years stamping out the Mau Mau, killing 10,000. The situation appeared ominous when former Mau Mau leader Jomo Kenyatta became independent Kenya's first prime minister. Many white settlers and Kenyatta loyalists alike expected a vengeful bloodbath to commence. But in his inaugural address, Kenyatta shocked the nation by telling the British who stayed in Kenya, "You forgive us, and we will forgive you." Kenyatta even asked for Christian burial when he died.[19]

Neville Langford-Smith, who later served as an Anglican bishop based in Nakuru, Kenya, noted how the atonement doctrine of reconciliation between man and God, emphasized during the revival, showed races and tribes how to reconcile. "We tend to underestimate the hatred of the European that is so widespread among Africans in Kenya," Langford-Smith said, "and it is a humbling and moving experience to be approached by an African brother who comes to apologize for having had this hatred, from which the Lord has now cleansed him."[20] Church Missionary Society general secretary Max Warren credited the East African Revival for preparing a Kenyan remnant to endure the Mau Mau persecution and preserve the church while nominal masses faded into the angry crowds.

"There were those for whom the joy of Christian life, the strength of Christian fellowship, and the 'burden' they felt for other men, were all caught up in their love for Jesus," Warren said. "So it is that the words 'Mau Mau' have become a battle honour of the church. It is no secret that when the real day of testing came with blood and flame and sword, it was the men and women of the

Revival Fellowships who saved the Church. That is literally true and needs no allowance for exaggeration."[21]

Ugandan bishop Festo Kivengere visited a convention gathering of 11,000 in Kenya shortly following the Mau Mau uprising. He watched as a Kikuyu taxi driver from Nairobi, shaking and weeping, confessed that during three years as a terrorist he killed at least sixty people. Nevertheless, he felt God's love and knew God had forgiven him of all his sins. Still, one incident troubled him. "But there may be a woman in this crowd whose husband I helped to hang in the bedroom, in front of her," he said. "Can such a woman forgive such a beast of a man?" Indeed, a woman approached him from the crowd, which hushed with anticipation. She reached out and grasped the hand of her husband's killer. "I forgave you that night, when my husband prayed for you," she said. "You are now my brother."[22]

Uganda's Moment of Truth

Nine Anglican bishops conferred together in a home near the cathedral on Namirembe Hill in Kampala, Uganda's capital. That morning they brainstormed how they could secure the release of Archbishop Janani Luwum. One day earlier, February 17, 1977, officers of President Idi Amin, a Muslim despot, had taken Luwum into custody. Suddenly a woman interrupted their meeting with terrible news from the morning paper: "Archbishop and Two Ministers Die in Motor Accident." Devastated, the bishops knew the fact was much worse than this journalistic fiction. Luwum and the other passengers did not try to seize control of the jeep, causing it to overturn, as the newspaper reported. In fact, the bishops recognized that the license plate in the newspaper photo belonged to a car that had crashed two weeks before. The television news that evening showed a different car and said it was the one Luwum died in. In truth, Amin had ordered Luwum's assassination. After authorities shot Luwum, they ran over his body with a car to make his death look like a traffic accident.

The first missionaries entered Uganda in 1877, one century before Amin killed Luwum. Almost from the beginning, martyrdom was the likely cost of conversion for new Christians. Only eight years after Christianity came to Uganda, a suspicious king ordered the murder of the first Anglican bishop sent from England. That same year, 1885, three boys ranging from eleven to fifteen years old became the first native Ugandan Christians killed for their faith. But they would be far from the last. Preparing for the church's centennial celebration in 1977, six actors rehearsed a play that would commemorate the Ugandan church's dramatic origins. They planned to portray the boy martyrs who gave their lives in 1885. Drama became reality when the lifeless bodies of these six men were discovered together in a field.

Uganda's history of revivals induced the rapid church growth that threatened authorities such as Amin who practiced other religions. But revival also steeled Uganda's church with resolve to endure its most difficult challenge under Amin. His regime started with a military coup in early 1971 that carried the support of many Ugandans, including Christians who were thankful for his promise of free elections. He spoke at a large pastors' conference, regularly received church officials who requested meetings, and even helped to mediate a dispute between leaders in the Church of Uganda.

Signs indicated Amin would not live up to his promise, though a supreme court judge and other revered national leaders began disappearing. Christians were jailed though they had broken no laws. Then the public executions started. Festo Kivengere witnessed an execution carried out by a firing squad before a silent crowd ordered to watch. One condemned man's parents served as evangelists in Kivengere's diocese. As they walked toward the stadium where they would be executed, the men told the bishop about their recent conversions. They radiated the joy of the Lord and asked Kivengere to tell their families not to worry, for they were going to be with Jesus. Despite handcuffs, they waved toward the crowd, who waved back. Then three shots felled them, sending them to be with their Lord.[23]

Supported by Saudi Arabia, Libya, and several other nations, Amin sought to remake Uganda into an Islamic haven.

Demographics complicated his ambitions. At the time, only 10 percent of Ugandans were Muslim, while between 60 and 75 percent claimed Christianity. Undaunted, Amin explored new depths of depravity. Hundreds of thousands of Christians died under his rule. But try as he might, Amin could not stop God from turning his murderous prisons into revival halls. Badly battered, the church welcomed signs of God's faithfulness.

"As danger and discomfort increased, there was a spiritual quickening," Kivengere wrote. "We saw people coming to fellowship meetings who had been absent a long time. There were deep repentances before God and reconciliations with the brethren. There was joy and praise in the Spirit as one and another found liberty. We read God's Word with an urgency of needing to know what He wanted us to do in our situation."[24]

More than 4,000 Christians braved Amin's threats and honored Luwum at his funeral in the Namirembe Hill cathedral on February 20, 1977. Afterward the persecution grew more severe. Church leaders facing imminent danger, including Kivengere, fled Uganda. But throngs of spiritual seekers crowded into the churches.

Even as Ugandan leaders such as Bishop Festo Kivengere were forced to flee, spiritual seekers crowded into churches. (Courtesy of the Billy Graham Evangelistic Association.)

Many nominal Christians converted as they realized the persecution might catch them next.[25]

Persecution doesn't always bring this clarifying perspective to the church and sow the seeds of revival. When the persecution is sufficiently systematic, severe, and sustained, as it was centuries ago in places such as modern-day Libya and Saudi Arabia, the church disperses and disappears. The persecution in Kenya and Uganda, however, failed to stamp out the flames of faith fanned by revival. A church already broken by its own sin and desperate need for a Savior is better positioned to withstand attack. Revival reaches Christians who recognize and admit publicly that God is their only hope.

"Revival doesn't come to respectable Christians," Kivengere wrote before the persecution chased him from Uganda. "If you think that because you're a good church member, or because you belong to such and such an organization, you're going to be revived, you had better forget it. The basis of revival is men and women shattered by their failures — aware that all is not well, helpless to do anything about it."[26]

But God can make all things well with the souls of Christians who lean on his grace. "The church is like our African grasslands, where I herded cattle as a boy," Kivengere said. "Huge fires roar over it, and the land looks black and dead. But immediately after the first rain, the grass springs up more luxuriantly than ever. The plains turn green and the cows fatten. No fire passing over the church can destroy the seeds of victorious faith. And the church in Uganda today is springing up, rich, green, and growing."[27]

What about Rwanda?

Likewise, the church continues to grow in Rwanda, but not without crises that have cast a long shadow on the revival. Even before 1960, there were signs that the revival had not fully healed long-standing tribal rivalries. Rwandan Hutus, traditionally servants to the ruling Tutsi, ended the monarchy and started a republic. The gospel message of liberation from sin had encouraged them to seek their freedom. But in the process, they bludgeoned anyone who tried to stop them from burning Tutsi homes and killing livestock. The Tutsi sought sanctuary in the missions. Joe Church, a friend to the deposed Tutsi monarch, fled to Uganda with thousands of other refugees. "The Gospel of the love of God, free to all alike, that we preached and practiced in our churches and hospitals and lived in our fellowships, seemed to be forgotten," Church wrote.[28] Several buildings at the Gahini mission were destroyed.

"The believers in Rwanda held true to their faith, but irreparable damage was done to the country, bitterness and hatred poisoning the relationship of the masses," Orr wrote. "The younger generation, unmoved by the Revival, grew up into apathy or antagonism. The ongoing Rwanda Revival, twenty-five years effective, suffered its worst setback."[29]

Sadly, far worse days would come. In 1994 at least 800,000 Rwandans, maybe even 1 million, died in one of the quickest, largest, and most gruesome genocides in human history. Once again, Hutu hatred flared against the Tutsi. And all this took place in one of the world's most thoroughly Christianized nations. As of 1991, 90 percent of Rwandans claimed Christian faith: 62 percent belonged to the Roman Catholic Church, 18 percent to Protestant churches, and 8 percent to the Seventh-day Adventist Church.[30]

Rwanda's revival history complicates the agonizing questions of how the genocide could have happened. It became clear in retrospect that when the revival faded, many churches failed to carry on the work of discipleship so that believers could still pursue sanctification. Church hierarchies grew wealthy and complacent. Prior commitments to tribal harmony gave way to Anglican leadership dominated by Hutus. During the genocide some priests even aided the killers. Christian leaders belatedly recognized the rot hidden by Rwanda's revival history. Roger Bowen, general secretary for Mid-Africa Ministry, the new name for the Rwanda Mission of the Church Missionary Society, identified weaknesses in the individualistic theology that undergirded the revival.

"The Church in Rwanda has operated with a very privatized and inadequate view of sin," Bowen said in 1995.

The challenge to repentance has usually focused on a fairly limited range of private morality—lying, stealing, adultery, drunkenness. However there is little awareness of the solidarities of sin that we are embedded in as members of society.... Ironically, the Revival doctrine of sin underestimates the power and depth of evil, and by focusing on personal/private morality is quite inadequate to tackle the hideous strength of structural evil and corporate sin manifested in an act of genocide.[31]

Weakened by the time of the genocide, the revival had changed many lives over the course of several decades. But it could not last forever, and it had not solved every problem. During a series of events that preceded the genocide, most church leaders remained silent. What business did they have interfering in political matters? Voices demanding revenge filled the void and incited the crowds. The Rwandan church's overly private focus limited how much it could equip believers who must demonstrate their faith publicly.

"What if?" questions have dogged the revival's proponents ever since the fateful events of 1994. While revival does not promise perpetual utopia, shouldn't we expect it to thwart mass murder? Maybe so, but revival can never supplant the need for consistent, faithful teaching and discipleship. Without this follow-up plan, revival can promote mountaintop spirituality ill equipped to survive the valleys of life. Today Rwanda is recovering, and the church has taken a leading role. President Paul Kagame has embraced pastor Rick Warren and named Rwanda the first Purpose Driven nation. Church leaders pray that the revival will resume so God may heal the ills that still ail their nation.

NOTES

1. J. E. Church, *Quest for the Highest: A Diary of the East African Revival* (Exeter, U.K.: Paternoster, 1981), 34.

2. Ibid., 51.

3. Richard K. MacMaster with Donald R. Jacobs, *A Gentle Wind of God: The Influence of the East Africa Revival* (Scottdale, Pa.: Herald Press, 2006), 27.

4. Ibid., 28–29.

5. Church, *Quest for the Highest*, 66.

6. MacMaster with Jacobs, *Gentle Wind of God*, 31.

7. Church, *Quest for the Highest*, 70.

8. Ibid., 136.

9. Joe Church, *Jesus Satisfies!* (Achimota, Ghana: Africa Christian Press, 1969), 39.

10. MacMaster with Jacobs, *Gentle Wind of God*, 49.

11. Church, *Quest for the Highest*, 194.

12. Ibid., 99.

13. Ibid.,126.

14. Ibid., 167.

15. J. Edwin Orr, *Evangelical Awakenings in Africa* (Minneapolis: Bethany Fellowship, 1975), 181.

16. Dorothy W. Smoker, *Ambushed by Love: God's Triumph in Kenya's Terror* (Fort Washington, Pa.: Christian Literature Crusade, 1993), 20.

17. Ibid., 21.

18. Orr, *Evangelical Awakenings in Africa*, 181–83.

19. Smoker, *Ambushed by Love*, 25.

20. Cited in MacMaster with Jacobs, *Gentle Wind of God*, 59.

21. Church, *Quest for the Highest*, 250.

22. Festo Kivengere, *When God Moves in Revival* (Wheaton, Ill.: Tyndale, 1973), 36.

23. Festo Kivengere with Dorothy Smoker, *I Love Idi Amin: The Story of Triumph under Fire in the Midst of Suffering and Persecution in Uganda* (Old Tappan, N.J.: Revell, 1977), 26.

24. Ibid., 18.

25. Ibid., 57.

26. Kivengere, *When God Moves in Revival*, 17.

27. Kivengere with Smoker, *I Love Idi Amin*, 13.

28. Church, *Quest for the Highest*, 252.

29. Orr, *Evangelical Awakenings in Africa*, 188.

30. Meg Guillebaud, *Rwanda: The Land God Forgot? Revival, Genocide, and Hope* (Grand Rapids: Monarch, 2002), 284.

31. Ibid., 323.

CHAPTER 7

KINGDOM FROM ABOVE

Henan, Manchurian, and Shantung Revivals, 1900s to 1930s
CHINA

Despite more than half a century of extensive missionary efforts, Protestant churches claimed a mere 37,000 members in China in 1889.[1] When the Boxer uprising unsettled China in 1900, Protestant membership still had not approached 100,000 in the world's most populous country. And it appeared as though Christianity would never take root when 189 Protestant missionaries and their families, along with many thousands of Chinese Christians, perished in the uprising.

Jonathan Goforth, a Canadian Presbyterian missionary, had served in China since 1887. Eagerly longing to see results, Goforth could not contain his disappointment that so few Chinese had embraced the gospel before the century turned. "In the early pioneer years I had buoyed myself with the assurance that a seed-time must always precede a harvest, and had, therefore, been content to persist in the apparently futile struggle," Goforth remembered. "But now thirteen years had passed, and the harvest seemed, if anything, farther away than ever."

Still, Goforth did not waver in his assurance that God planned to use him. "I felt sure that there was something larger ahead of me, if I only had the vision to see what it was, and the faith to grasp it."[2] That faith was severely tested when he led his family to safety and fled China in 1900. The Boxer riots, which targeted foreigners, overtook them in a small town. His wife, Rosalind, vividly remembered the bloody day in Hsintien. Of Jonathan's injuries she wrote:

> One blow from a two-handed sword struck him on the neck with great force, showing the blow was meant to kill, but the whole wide blunt edge struck his neck leaving only a wide bruise two-thirds around the neck. The thick pith helmet he was wearing was slashed almost to pieces, one blow severing the inner leather band just over the temple, went a fraction of an inch short of being fatal for the skin was not touched. His left arm which was kept raised to protect his head, was slashed to the bone in several places. A terrible blow from behind struck the back of his head, denting in the skull so deeply, that, later, doctors said it was a miracle the skull was not cleft in two. This blow felled him to the ground. It was then he seemed to hear clearly a voice saying—"Fear not! They are praying for you!" Struggling to his feet, he was struck down again by a club.[3]

Believing they had killed Jonathan, the mob allowed Rosalind and the children to leave. But they had not finished the job. When the mob moved on, local Muslim villagers hid Jonathan and his family and offered them food and water. Still wearing their bloodied clothes, they eventually reached Shanghai. They returned to Canada and nursed their wounds. But the Goforth family returned to China near the end of 1901 when the uprising had died down. In the meantime, China had changed. Surprisingly, Christianity found a far better reception after the Boxer incident. The church had grown stronger and bolder by enduring the persecution. China Inland Mission workers testified to 802 baptisms in Henan Province alone in 1903.[4] The Protestant church across China grew rapidly to 178,000 members by 1906.[5]

Divine Discontent

Still, Goforth longed to see God do even greater things. Stories of revival in Wales and India whetted his appetite. He longed to see revival. In 1905 a friend in India sent him a booklet that included snippets of Charles Finney's autobiography and lectures on revival. "It was the final something which set me on fire," Goforth said.[6] He was convinced by Finney's argument that just as farmers must follow the laws of nature, so must revivalists know the laws of spiritual harvesting. His reliance on Finney deepened when another friend loaned him a full copy of the famed revivalist's autobiography in 1906.

"We wish to state most emphatically as our conviction that God's revival may be at hand when we will and where we will," Goforth later wrote, echoing Finney and evangelist D. L. Moody. In the East as in the West, whether suddenly or prolonged over weeks, revival comes to those who follow God's will, Goforth

Jonathan and Rosalind Goforth, undaunted by a nearly lethal attack during the Boxer uprising in 1900, returned to China. (Courtesy of the Archives of the Billy Graham Center, Wheaton, Illinois.)

believed. Anyone who asks may receive Pentecost's blessings. "Our reading of the Word of God makes it inconceivable to us that the Holy Spirit should be willing, even for a day, to delay His work," Goforth argued. "We may be sure that, where there is a lack of the fullness of God, it is ever due to man's lack of faith and obedience. If God the Holy Spirit is not glorifying Jesus Christ in the world today, as at Pentecost, it is we who are to blame. After all, what is revival but simply the Spirit of God fully controlling the surrendered life? It must always be possible, then, when man yields. The sin of unyieldedness, alone, can keep us from revival."[7]

Goforth traveled to Pyongyang in 1907 and saw the aftermath of Korea's revival, which had been likewise stirred by reports of awakening in Wales and India. The ambitious missionary became even more deeply convicted that if the one true God of the whole world sent revival to these far-flung locales, he would send revival to China. Visiting Korea, Goforth was impressed by the early-morning prayer meetings, sacrificial giving, zeal for Scripture, and willingness to suffer for the sake of Christ. Goforth wrote: "A burning zeal to make known the merits of the Saviour was a special mark of the Church at Pentecost. The same is not less true of the Korean Church. It was said that the heathen complained that they could not endure the persecution of the Christians. They were evermore telling of the strong points of their Saviour. Some declared they would have to sell out and move to some district where there were no Christians, in order to get rest."[8]

When Goforth returned home to China's Henan Province, accounts of the Korean revival inspired fellow missionaries and the Chinese alike. Crowds were riveted by his stories of hidden sins confessed, rivalries healed, and masses saved. Yet Goforth did not see revival in China until the Lord dealt with one lingering conflict. Goforth had felt convicted about the need to reconcile with a fellow missionary, but he hadn't yet acted. He was sure he was in the right, and the other missionary had even apologized. But Goforth could not put the issue to rest, despite perceiving nearly audible commands from God. Finally, in the middle of a talk, Goforth resolved to reconcile. He was sure that God would not go with him on an upcoming tour of mission stations unless he made things right. The seemingly simple resolution brought immediate changes. Without telling anyone of this silent commitment, Goforth saw the crowd's demeanor change. When people stood to pray, they began weeping instead and could not continue. Never before in twenty years in Henan had the missionaries seen such genuine penitence from the Chinese.

No one gushed over Goforth's speaking skills, as if he could subliminally compel audience reactions. But crowds heeded his heartfelt, plain-spoken pleas for confession and repentance. They shared his confidence that the Holy Spirit would work. They followed his admonitions to pray, trust the Bible, and exalt Jesus. His missionary colleagues agreed to pray for revival simultaneously every day, wherever they found themselves at 4:00 p.m.

Manchurian Candidates for Revival

Goforth headed for Mukden, Manchuria, in February 1908. When he arrived, he was disheartened to learn that no one there had prayed for him. His host missionary family even showed disdain for traditional theology and had no interest in revival. The Scottish and Irish Presbyterians would not cooperate. Goforth despaired and brought his concerns before the Lord. Then he heard God say, "Is it your work or Mine? Can I not do a sovereign work?"[9] Indeed, God can, and he did. During one meeting, a local elder confessed publicly that he had embezzled church money. Plagued by guilt, he couldn't sleep the evening after Goforth's first talk. Another confessed to adultery and trying to murder his wife. The church began praying for members who left the fold and had not returned. Soon hundreds of so-called backsliders came home. Some admitted that they were not true believers previously. The host missionaries could hardly believe their eyes. They remarked how the revival resembled the Scottish awakening in 1859.

Goforth's spirit lifted even higher when he learned that thousands of Koreans had prayed specifically for revival at his next destination, Liaoyang. Once again, Goforth witnessed an outpouring of confession. Groups of revived Christians traveled the countryside spreading the gospel and sharing about how the Lord had awakened them. When he traveled to Kwangning, a stoic group of Presbyterians prayed with newfound fervor. Goforth noticed one man, strong and smart, but clearly pained by something. After a few days, the man finally spoke up.

"O God, you know what my position is—a preacher," the man said.

> When I came to these meetings I determined that, come what would, I would keep my sins covered up. I knew that if I confessed my sins it would bring disgrace not only upon myself but upon my family and my church. But I can't keep it hidden any longer. I have committed adultery.... But that is not all. In one of the out-stations a deacon committed a horrible sin which hindered Thy cause. My plain duty was to report the affair to the missionary, but the deacon bought me a fur garment, and I accepted it and it sealed my lips. But I can't wear it any longer.[10]

The pastor ripped off the fur and threw it away. That meeting alone, filled with many such confessions and prayers for mercy, continued for six hours. Even non-Christians noticed the meeting and visited to see the revival for themselves. Many of them followed suit and asked God to show them mercy. When Goforth visited Chinchow, missionary Dr. Walter Phillips was skeptical. His temperament loathed "revival hysterics." But after visiting two meetings, Phillips gained a new perspective.

"At once, on entering the church, one was conscious of something unusual," he said.

> The place was crowded to the door, and tense, reverent attention sat on every face. The very singing was vibrant with new joy and vigour.... The people knelt for prayer, silent at first, but soon one here and another there began to pray aloud. The voices grew and gathered volume and blended into a great wave of united supplication that swelled till it was almost a roar, and died down again into an undertone of weeping. Now

I understood why the floor was so wet—it was wet with pools of tears! The very air seemed electric—I speak in all serious-ness—and strange thrills coursed up and down one's body.

Then above the sobbing, in strained, choking tones, a man began to make public confession. Words of mine will fail to describe the awe and terror and pity of these confessions. It was not so much the enormity of the sins disclosed, or the depths of iniquity sounded, that shocked one.... It was the agony of the penitent, his groans and cries, and voice shaken with sobs; it was the sight of men forced to their feet, and, in spite of their struggles, impelled, as it seemed, to lay bare their hearts that moved one and brought the smarting tears to one's own eyes. Never have I experienced anything more heart breaking, more nerve racking than the spectacle of those souls stripped naked before their fellows.[11]

Uprising Survivors Learn to Forgive

It was a miracle that even a small Christian community survived in Shinminfu to greet Goforth. During the Boxer uprising, the Shinminfu church lost fifty-four martyrs. Unbowed, the church compiled a list of 250 people who conspired to kill the Christians. The Christians waited for a day to come when they could exact revenge. An evangelist whose father was murdered confessed to Goforth that he could not forgive. He pledged never to rest until he avenged his father by killing the killer. Nine boys who lost family members admitted that they wanted revenge but asked the church to pray that they would find grace and forgive. The boys' willingness to move on left an impression on the elder evangelist, who said:

When I went home after the service I thought of how the devil would be sure to take advantage of my example and put you boys to ridicule. People would say that you were too young to know your own minds. Then they would point to me as an intelligent man who surely ought to know his own mind, and say "he doesn't believe in that foolish talk about forgiving one's enemies." So, lest the devil should mislead you, I have bought these nine hymn books and I am going to present one to each of you, in the hope that every time you open it to praise God from its pages you will recall how that I, an evangelist, received from Him grace to forgive the murderer of my father.[12]

When the evangelist finished, the crowd tore up the list of 250 names and stomped on the remains. If the revival brought peace to the church in Shinminfu, perhaps it could help the beleaguered church in Shansi, where the persecution of 1900 was even worse. In the days of the Boxer uprising, the brutal Shansi governor Yu Hsien prepared to execute a group of missionaries. An adolescent girl spoke up like Jesus, Peter, and John before her, and asked the governor what wrong the missionaries had committed. "Haven't our doctors come from far-off lands to give their lives for your people?" the girl asked him. "Many with hopeless disease have been healed; some who were blind received their sight, and health and happiness have been brought into thousands of your homes because of what our doctors have done. Is it because of this good that has been done that you are going to kill us?"[13] She spoke a brief while longer as the governor squirmed. But a soldier quickly ended the courageous display when he grabbed the girl's hair and cut off her head. That day, fifty-nine missionaries were martyred. More than a hundred missionaries in Shansi ultimately lost their lives during the ordeal.

By the time Goforth visited in 1908, it was obvious the church had not recovered. Shansi's church members had earned a poor reputation among their neighbors. Some church members abused their wives. Others defrauded business partners. But in response to Goforth's visit, these struggling Christians began making amends with those they had wronged. Even one of the Boxer persecution's backslidden heroes, named Kuo, repented of the drunken rage he sometimes exhibited in the years since 1900. Kuo couldn't explain to Goforth exactly how or why he changed. But suddenly he felt a burning as if he would burst into flames unless he confessed and repented of his sins.[14] Repentance and restitution characterized other revival outbreaks, including on in Xinghua, Fujian Province, where awakened Christians handed over opium pipes and a two-edged assassin's sword.[15]

Back in Goforth's home station in Changteh, the revival met surprising resistance. While Goforth was traveling to other missionary posts, some of his colleagues began to cast doubt on the stories that came streaming back to them. After a week of revival meetings, a missionary doctor came forward and aired his doubts. The doctor doubted the revival's origins with the Holy Spirit. Instead, he believed Goforth somehow hypnotized his audiences. Yet seven days of seeing became believing for this skeptic. Only God could inspire such a revival by sending his Holy Spirit. The missionary apologized to Goforth before asking the crowd to forgive him for believing they had fallen under one mere mortal's spell.

On the other end of the spectrum, Goforth rebuked missionaries who expected revival to automatically erupt when he visited. An English missionary, Miss Gregg, told her Chinese friends to anticipate many blessings when Goforth visited Hwailu. But during Goforth's meetings, she was disappointed to see that the same rivalries persisted as offended parties refused to confess and repent. She began to doubt whether she could trust God. So Goforth confronted her.

> Miss Gregg, I think I am beginning to see where the hindrance lies. You had heard how God had moved at Changteh and Paotingfu and elsewhere, and you made up your mind that He must do a similar work here in Hwailu or so disappoint you that you would throw up your work and go back to England. In other words, as far as you were concerned, God had no option. He must please you in your own way or else lose your service. Remember that God is sovereign. He can never lay aside His sovereign will and authority.[16]

When Goforth stopped his rebuke, a man burst in and reported that the revival had broken out. Still, his point was valid. No matter the so-called laws of revival, God will not be manipulated.

Monsen without Pretense

Just as he worked seemingly wherever Goforth traveled, the Lord moved other missionaries to pray for revival. Norwegian missionary Marie Monsen caught a vision for how the Lord could work as she read biographies of the great evangelist and friend to orphans George Müller and China Inland Mission founder Hudson Taylor. When she read the book of Acts, she saw how her pioneering mission work resembled the apostle Paul's great missionary journeys through the Roman world. News of the Korean revival in 1907 brought Monsen great encouragement. "Oh, to be able to go there and bring back some glowing coals to our own field!" Monsen exclaimed.[17]

Along with praying for revival, Monsen identified Bible study as a key component of preparation to see God work in mighty ways. Just when you need the help, Monsen believed, hymns and Bible passages you have learned will come to mind. "The Spirit uses the Word" became one of her catchphrases. But as Monsen reflected during her first furlough, she felt like God needed to strip her of any pretense that she could do this missionary work by her own education and training. She remembered, "The Lord was seeking to mould a missionary who would know inwardly that she was one of the chosen 'things that are not,' who must learn to reckon with God and rely on His power."[18] A second furlough brought no breakthrough. Upon returning to China for a third stint, Monsen found like-minded women who shared her longing to meet the Lord in prayer and see him work according to his promises. Yet revival still did not come.

Turmoil forced Monsen and other missionaries to evacuate their interior posts and find safe haven on the coasts in 1927. Nationalist Chinese, aggrieved by treaties that favored the West, took out their frustrations on missionaries.[19] After a brief stint in Shanghai, Monsen headed for Manchuria, site of the 1908 revival. Standing in for a Chinese pastor who was late in arriving, Monsen spoke to crowds ripe for a revival harvest. Each time she visited another missionary post, Monsen put her life at risk. In these days, an ineffective central government could not secure the vast nation, so travel was treacherous, especially for a single woman. During one trip from Tientsin to Hwanghsien, pirates held Monsen captive for twenty-three days.

Monsen reported:

> Just before daylight, I heard pistol shots all over the ship, and I knew immediately what we were in for. The words came to me: "This is a trial of your faith." I remember the thrill of joy that went through me at the thought of it. I was immediately reminded of the word that I had been using much in years gone by, in Isaiah 41:10, and I will read it to you as I had been reading it down on the Honan plains, "Fear not, Marie, for I am with thee; be not dismayed, Marie, for I am thy God; I will strengthen thee, Marie, yea I will uphold thee, Marie, with the right hand of my righteousness."[20]

Armed with these words from God, Monsen viewed the bondage as merely another opportunity to share the gospel with a new audience.

The confinement delayed Monsen's visit to see old Southern Baptist missionary friends in Shantung Province until 1929. She had long anticipated this reunion. "They were a group of steady, well-trained, godly, warm-hearted missionaries and they had prayed for revival for years," she said. "It was like coming to a vast field fully ripe for harvesting. It was the harvesting work we were to do together."[21] Indeed, Southern Baptist missionaries wrote home to describe the outpouring on their churches in North China. Writing from Chefoo in 1932, one observer identified the catalysts for revival as "earnest prayer, faith in God, Bible teaching, and much preaching on sin and kindred subjects." Some of the revival's manifestations may have surprised Baptists back home.

> Numbers of Christians and churches are being revived; restitution of money is being made; tithes of the Lord held back are being brought forward; sins confessed to God and to those who have been wronged; sick are being healed; devils cast out; men and women, boys and girls are preaching with a power

hitherto not known; hundreds are crying for mercy and are being saved.[22]

That same year, a missionary observed changes in Pingtu county, a densely populated and notoriously unsafe part of Shantung. A few years earlier, missionaries wisely declined to stay overnight in a notorious Pingtu village. Otherwise, they risked theft or even kidnapping by bandits who might hold them for ransom or even kill them. But the revival transformed the community. Missionaries could sleep with their doors wide open. That spring they baptized forty new Christians in the town.[23]

Along with these evangelistic results, many wayward church members truly believed the gospel for the first time. Chao Te San had left a strong impression on his teachers at the Hwanghsien mission. When he grew up, he became a successful businessman building roads and managing railroads. Retired in Peiping, he still wielded influence in politics and the financial sector. But he had forsaken the way of the Lord. Though he had taken a concubine, his wife convinced him to attend a church service during the revival. He complained about the preaching but returned for another meeting. This time he began to be convicted about his sins and wanted to put things right. After a few months, he believed the gospel. He sent away his concubine, giving her money for schooling, and began to evangelize his business friends. He used the railroad to visit former colleagues and tell them about Jesus Christ. As the revival progressed, he supported and traveled along with a small group of uneducated, illiterate evangelists.[24]

All around, reports suggested a remarkable awakening. Monsen rejoiced to see the long-awaited revival. Fulfilling an earlier dream, she visited Korea in 1930 and stood in the very room where missionaries gathered for daily prayer. Their example still inspired her. "Here they were stripped of all that was of self, till they were 'unprofitable servants' in their own eyes and 'declared themselves bankrupt.' Here they unitedly resolved to continue in prayer until they were given a revival like the revival in Wales and in India. Their request was granted."[25]

Students Step Forward

Monsen and Goforth had plenty of company on the road as they headlined short conferences that often erupted in revival. Given the political turmoil inside and around China, it was crucial that indigenous leaders began taking responsibility for the church. The revival helped them do just that in the years leading up to the Sino-Japanese War in 1937.[26] Gustav Carlberg served as president of Lutheran Theological Seminary at Shekow in Hupeh Province. He wrote in 1936 that the revival enabled Chinese leaders to begin taking over. "No longer do our Chinese Christians feel that the church is an imported institution. God visited them; He has given them the same blessings as He has given to the church in other lands; they have had the same experiences. They now feel themselves to be members of the church universal in their own right. This gives them an interest in the church and a desire to further its activities as never before."[27]

One of the first Chinese leaders to reach prominence was Ding Limei. Born in 1871, he graduated from Calvin Meeter's Christian academy in Shadong, which later became Shadong Union College. Dubbed the "Moody of China," he found receptive audiences for the gospel in schools. Many of these students converted under Ding in the revival would become pillars of the flourishing indigenous Chinese church.[28]

Students were catalysts for revival in several venues across China. From his post at the Lutheran seminary, Carlberg heard revival reports come in from different provinces. The news excited some faculty and students while others remained cynical, waiting to see for themselves. In the fall of 1932, a student named Hsü Süeh Djon enrolled in the seminary's two-year program. He had been transformed during his time in Hsüchang, where revival had broken out. Carlberg knew Hsü as a middle school student and wasn't impressed.

"At that time he showed little inclination toward spiritual things, and even less inclination to study, but God sometimes makes use of seemingly impossible material to fashion special instruments for His own use."[29] Indeed, Hsü devoted himself to prayer and introducing other students to the risen, powerful Jesus Christ.

Revival swept the campus in January 1933, beginning with a board of directors meeting, of all things. Board member and pastor Ai Shui Sheng was spiritually awakened and filled with new zeal. He began meeting with students and organized them in prayer groups that stretched late into evening as they confronted sin, prompted by reading passages such as Romans 1 together. They repented of sin such as greed, gossip, slander, and arrogance (Rom. 1:28–32).

"I had never previously understood why there should be so many and so detailed catalogs of sin in the Bible, but now I perceived they had a very practical use," Carlberg wrote. "God knew what He was about when He caused the Bible to be written just the way it is. Scripture is indeed, 'profitable for reproof and correction,' when occasion requires."[30]

More than half the seminary's students participated in the revival by repenting of their sins, a precursor to spiritual reawakening. But the students hardly kept the revival to themselves.

Carlberg said:

> Many of them have now gone forth into the great harvest field to garner souls for the Lord of the harvest. What a satisfaction to know that these men go forth, not only equipped with a head-knowledge, and with other equipment necessary for the work of a pastor, but that they have been specially equipped by God with a living experience of his grace in their lives, and a special anointing of His Spirit of power, with which to cope with the arduous details of their responsible positions![31]

In the short run, the revival also changed the school's feel. Students regarded their classmates and professors with more respect. Discipline problems nearly disappeared. And outside observers noticed the new passion in the students' prayers. One of China's most well-known and controversial leaders also experienced revival in a school. Wang Mindao was born in 1900, the year of the Boxer uprising, in which his father, a medical doctor, died. Wang planned to become a government official and was teaching in a Presbyterian school when he experienced a personal revival in 1920. Through him, the revival spread to many students. But his enthusiasm waned when he returned home for three years.

"Persecution in the home, misunderstanding on the part of friends, all came upon me at once like a storm," Wang said. "I did not know how to meet all this. When I looked around, there was no help. I could only pray and read the Bible in a small room by myself. Praise the Lord, at this time He opened my eyes to behold the mystery of His salvation. God gave also joy, hope, and glory. The Bible became my precious treasury and daily food. All my former ambition, great name, education, all became like a vanishing cloud."[32]

In 1920 Wang founded the Christian Tabernacle in Beijing, one of China's largest churches. His high profile made him a target of Communist officials following World War II. Wang further aggravated them by declining to join the official Three-Self Patriotic Movement. He spent two terms in jail, the latter ending in 1980.

After decades of sometimes vicious persecution, China's booming church emerged in the 1980s as a powerful force in society. Scholars have observed the characteristics of revival in this reemergence.

> Older Christians renewed themselves and proudly reestablished their public identity as believers; new, younger converts produced dynamic traveling evangelists and revival leaders who matured growing churches, especially in the rural areas; and a strong stress on the Holy Spirit in much of the revivalism of the 1980s called to mind the prominent Pentecostal strand in revivalism after 1920.[33]

The Chinese church's stress today recalls Goforth's belief that spiritual power and growth come not by human effort but by the Holy Spirit. He believed the Holy Spirit works in revival by illumining the Scriptures. Therefore, Goforth strongly resisted modernist efforts that he believed undermined biblical authority.

"There never has been a revival except where there have been Christian men and women thoroughly believing in and wholeheartedly pleading the promises of God," Goforth said.

The Sword of the Spirit, which is the Word of God, is the only weapon which has ever been mightily used in revival. Where it has been given for what it claims to be, the Word of God has always been like a sharp, two-edged sword, like fire, and like a hammer that breaketh the rock in pieces. When Luther got the Scriptures translated into German, that country was lost to Rome. Moody did not possess the learning of the schools, but he did know his Bible; and it is certain that the world has never known and doubtful if it ever will know, his equal as an apostle of souls.[34]

Ever the advocate for revival, Goforth believed the church bears responsibility for ensuring that nothing, not least our best efforts, hinder the Holy Spirit's work.

"Brethren, the Spirit of God is with us still," Goforth exhorted. "Pentecost is yet within our grasp. If revival is being withheld from us it is because some idols remain still enthroned; because we still insist on placing our reliance on human schemes; because we still refuse to face the unchangeable truth that 'it is not by might, but BY MY SPIRIT.'"[35]

NOTES

1. Daniel H. Bays, "Christian Revival in China, 1900–1937," in *Modern Christian Revivals*, ed. Edith L. Blumhofer and Randall Balmer (Chicago: University of Illinois Press, 1993), 161.

2. Jonathan Goforth, *"By My Spirit"* (London: Marshall, Morgan & Scott, 1929), 23.

3. Rosalind Goforth, *Goforth of China* (Grand Rapids: Zondervan, 1937), 135.

4. Paul Hattaway, *Henan: The Galilee of China* (Carlisle, Cumbria, UK: Piquant, 2009), 47.

5. Bays, "Christian Revival in China," 162.

6. Goforth, *"By My Spirit,"* 24.

7. Ibid., 180–81.

8. Jonathan Goforth, *When the Spirit's Fire Swept Korea* (Grand Rapids: Zondervan, 1943), 17.

9. Ibid., 35.

10. Ibid., 47.

11. Ibid., 55.

12. Ibid., 59.

13. Ibid., 63.

14. Ibid., 68.

15. Lian Xi, *Redeemed by Fire: The Rise of Popular Christianity in Modern China* (New Haven, Conn.: Yale University Press, 2010), 88.

16. Goforth, *When the Spirit's Fire Swept Korea*, 127.

17. Marie Monsen, *The Awakening: Revival in China, a Work of the Holy Spirit*, trans. Joy Guinness (London: China Inland Mission, 1963), 28.

18. Ibid., 32.

19. Xi, *Redeemed by Fire*, 95.

20. Mary K. Crawford, *The Shantung Revival* (Shanghai: China Baptist Publication Society, 1933), 1–2.

21. Monsen, *Awakening*, 81.

22. Crawford, *Shantung Revival*, 26–27.

23. Ibid., 34.

24. Ibid., 64.

25. Monsen, *Awakening*, 88.

26. Xi, *Redeemed by Fire*, 98.

27. Gustav Carlberg, *China in Revival* (Rock Island, Ill.: Augustana Book Concern, 1936), 243.

28. Mark Shaw, *Global Awakening: How 20th-Century Revivals Triggered a Christian Revolution* (Downers Grove, Ill.: InterVarsity, 2010), 186.

29. Carlberg, *China in Revival*, 155.

30. Ibid., 156.

31. Ibid., 157.

32. Ibid., 54.

33. Bays, "Christian Revival in China," 175.

34. Goforth, *"By My Spirit,"* 185.

35. Ibid., 189.

CHAPTER 8

FIRST COMES WAR, THEN COMES REVIVAL

Evangelical Boom, 1940s to 1950s
NORTH AMERICA

For decades American Christians who recalled earlier awakenings had prayed for revival but had seen no results. Fellow believers told them not to expect another awakening because this world would only grow worse and worse until Jesus Christ returned. After all, just look at the mainline Protestant denominations. Once they were growing, filled with men and women who believed the Bible and trusted in God's promises. Now, in the 1940s, their teachers found flaws in Scripture and doubted whether God really meant what he said. The situation outside the church offered no comfort either. The economy was in shambles. Demagogues around the world declared imminent vengeance upon all they perceived had wronged them.

Still, a few could make out a faint outline of hope off in the distance. Doesn't despair precede revival? Don't Christians begin to understand their absolute need for God when all seems lost? As contemporary events discouraged them, American evangelicals in the 1930s looked to their history for inspiration. They hoped that by reading stories of past revivals, they might gain inspiration to pray and work for awakening in their own day. Maybe the end would come soon, but God would never abandon his people. If they would turn from their sins and seek his face, perhaps God would once again send revival.

Harold John Ockenga had lived through some of the most discouraging, contentious recent events in American church life. When his mentor, J. Gresham Machen, left Princeton Seminary, Ockenga followed him to Philadelphia, where Machen founded Westminster Theological Seminary. As recently as the beginning of the twentieth century, Princeton was still a beacon of top-flight conservative Protestant scholarship. Machen, a New Testament professor, inherited the Princeton legacy from such greats as Charles Hodge (1797–1878) and B. B. Warfield (1851–1921). But Princeton had become a political flash point in debates over the direction of the Northern Presbyterian Church. When the denomination reorganized Princeton in 1929, Machen and several other faculty departed, finding the situation untenable.

When Ockenga became pastor of Boston's Park Street Church in 1936, he inherited one of the most famous pulpits in America. Founded in 1809, Park Street Church stored gunpowder during the War of 1812. Leading abolitionist William Lloyd Garrison gave his first antislavery sermon at Park Street on July 4, 1829. Three years later on Independence Day, "My Country 'Tis of Thee" was first sung by Park Street children. Not just any pastor could step into this prominent position. But Ockenga was up to the task. Outside his Park Street ministry, Ockenga would go on to help found several enduring evangelical institutions, including Fuller Theological Seminary, *Christianity Today* magazine, Gordon-Conwell Theological Seminary, and the National Association of Evangelicals. From his vantage point with the NAE, organized in April 1942, Ockenga could see the hopeful outline of revival become more clearly defined.

"The most hopeful factor in the National Association of Evangelicals for United Action is the revival spirit which has characterized its convention and rallies," Ockenga wrote in September 1942. "In every place those present have been bowed down before the Spirit of God in prayer, confession and intercession. Why could not this be the vanguard in the movement of revival? With purity in Apostolic Christian doctrine, with unity of endeavor among evangelicals, and with a new anointing of Divine love, we believe that it will be such a leadership. Let us pray to that end."[1]

Youth Turn to Christ

Even as World War II continued to rage, evidence of revival mounted. Chicagoland Youth for Christ, started by Torrey Johnson, packed Chicago Stadium for its Victory Rally on October 21, 1944. Evangelist Merv Rosell preached, and future Billy Graham crusade soloist George Beverly Shea sang. Graham himself preached at similar gatherings around the country just a few years later. Thousands upon thousands of youth responded to evangelistic appeals. During Youth for Christ's first annual convention in 1945, leaders drew up a constitution that recognized a "visitation of the Spirit of God in convicting and regenerating power among the youth, such as has not been seen in recent times."[2] These events gathered together evangelicals who often shared more in common with one another than members of their own churches or mainline denominations. Many would become leaders of the coming evangelical revival. But they cut their teeth with Youth for Christ.

"Its explosive growth was breathtaking, its global vision was ahead of its time, and its influence surprised even its most ardent supporters," historian Garth Rosell writes. "With rare exception, the cities with the strongest Youth for Christ presence in the 1940s became the cities most deeply touched by the revivals of the 1950s."[3]

Graham, Youth for Christ's first full-time worker, displayed evident gifting. But he had only recently graduated from Wheaton College in 1943, and he did not pursue advanced theological training. So he was jolted by correspondence from his close friend and fellow evangelist Chuck Templeton, who studied at Princeton Theological Seminary, as they talked in 1948 and 1949. Since Machen's departure at the height of the modernist/fundamentalist debates, Princeton had fallen in line with other seminaries teaching the higher critical methods of biblical interpretation. As a Princeton student, Templeton began doubting the authority of Scripture. In his private reading, Graham too had been unprepared for the theological dilemmas posed by renowned twentieth-century scholars Karl Barth and Reinhold Neibuhr. Confusing matters, Graham believed these neo-orthodox theologians invested familiar theological terminology with new definitions. And like Templeton,

Graham began to wonder whether the Bible's seeming contradictions could be reconciled, and whether he could trust the Bible as speaking authoritatively and accurately about God. Searching for answers, Graham examined the Bible's internal testimony, turning to passages such as 2 Timothy 3:16; 2 Peter 1:21; and Matthew 24:25. These passages indicated a high standard for biblical authority, but Graham still doubted.

These doubts carried high stakes for Graham, already serving Northwestern Bible and Missionary Training School in Minneapolis since 1948 as the youngest college president in the country. Founded by fundamentalist pastor William Bell Riley, Northwestern's doctrinal statement clearly advocated belief in God's infallible Word. Plus, Graham and his team were planning evangelistic meetings for Los Angeles, their largest citywide campaign to date.

Henrietta Mears advised several young evangelical leaders, including Billy Graham and Bill Bright. (Photo courtesy of Gospel Light. Used with permission.)

Despite his experience with Youth for Christ, Graham had only led two such citywide events. One targeted friendly Grand Rapids, Michigan, but a disappointing campaign in Altoona, Pennsylvania, only reinforced his lingering suspicions about biblical authority.

Plagued by doubt, Graham did not look forward to fulfilling his obligation to speak for the College Briefing Conference, held annually at Forest Home, a Los Angeles–area retreat center. The conference was convened by Henrietta Mears, director of religious education at First Presbyterian Church of Hollywood. In just three years with the church, Mears presided over a tenfold increase in Sunday school enrollment for all ages, from 450 to 4,500. Mears recruited an all-star cast of evangelical speakers, including J. Edwin Orr, the historian of revivals who had been recently awarded his doctorate from Oxford University. Orr and Graham had met in Florida in 1940, and Graham visited Orr in Oxford in 1947, when they prayed together in John Wesley's bedroom for another Great Awakening.[4] On the spot, Orr walked Graham through a brief history of revivals in the previous two centuries, showing the Southern evangelist how the Lord had mightily used young, ordinary believers who offered themselves in God's service. The two men would go on to serve together with Mears on the initial board of directors for Campus Crusade for Christ, founded by Mears's protégé Bill Bright.

During the College Briefing Conference, Graham felt tugged between Mears, a brilliant woman who trusted the Bible, and Templeton, who chided Graham for failing to catch up with the times and abandon his simplistic interpretation of the Bible. Alone one evening, Graham considered that Jesus himself recognized the Hebrew Scriptures as historical. "As that night wore on, my heart became heavily burdened," Graham remembered.

> Could I trust the Bible? With the Los Angeles Campaign galloping toward me, I had to have an answer. If I could not trust the Bible, I could not go on. I would have to quit the school presidency. I would have to leave pulpit evangelism. I was only thirty years of age. It was not too late to become a dairy farmer. But that night I believed with all my heart that the God who had saved my soul would never let go of me.

Graham walked around the picturesque Forest Home facilities, encircled by the San Bernadino Mountains. He knelt down in the woods and prayed.

> O God! There are many things in this book I do not understand. There are many problems with it for which I have no solution. There are many seeming contradictions. There are some areas in it that do not seem to correlate with modern science. I can't answer some of the philosophical and psychological questions Chuck and others are raising.

But Graham didn't end his prayer with this earnest confession. He pressed forward for resolution. "Father, I am going to accept this as Thy Word—by *faith*! I'm going to allow faith to go beyond my intellectual questions and doubts, and I will believe this to be Your inspired Word."[5]

Old-Fashioned Holy Ghost Revival

While Graham wrestled with God, churches around Los Angeles asked God to turn the upcoming evangelistic campaign into a revival. Historian Joel Carpenter identified about 800 such prayer groups in Southern California. "The evangelical forces of the city were mobilized as never before," Carpenter writes.[6] The man most responsible for these prayer groups was onetime Missouri Synod Lutheran pastor Armin Gesswein. Beginning in 1941 and 1942, he organized the Ministers' Prayer Fellowship for Revival in Los Angeles. Gesswein had seen the Norwegian revival in person in 1937 and 1938 and brought this zeal back across the Atlantic. These prayer meetings became a key rallying point for believers who would welcome the later revivals near the end of the decade. Orr likened them to the businessmen's prayer meetings in 1857–58, especially in how they avoided controversy and united Christians across opposing views on soteriology, polity, and baptism. They somehow also managed to overcome divisions over Pentecostal teaching on the second blessing and whether evangelicals should strictly separate from liberals. As the pastors prayed together, "theory was abandoned for a practical ecumenicity of seeking together for spiritual revival."[7]

Supported by prayer and emboldened with newfound confidence in the Scriptures, Graham pressed on with the Los Angeles campaign. He warned of the coming judgment in his first sermon, "We Need Revival." Graham thundered, "God Almighty is going to bring judgment upon this city unless people repent and believe—unless God sends an old-fashioned, heaven-sent, Holy Ghost revival."[8] He punctuated the end of every description of what ails America with the refrain "We need revival!"

Aided by favorable media coverage of celebrity conversions, Graham's tent meetings lasted eight weeks, attracting hundreds of thousands. Evangelistic meetings do not necessarily result in revival, but the turnout galvanized preexisting revival movements around Los Angeles. Like other revivalists claiming the twin legacy of Finney and Edwards, Graham walked a fine line between self-promotion and dependence on God. One observer wrote:

All possible hindrances to the working of the Holy Spirit were removed during the campaign. Applause was kept at a bare minimum. There was little instrumental music or singing of choruses. Beverly Shea concentrated on the old gospel songs which had been used of God so greatly in the past. Cliff Barrows centered his song leading and programming around the hymns of revival of days past, using as a theme song, "Send a Great Revival in My Soul."[9]

Despite his hunger to see the Lord work in great power, Orr had discouraged Graham from holding the meetings. He believed Graham should wait to allow the Spirit to continue preparing the way. Afterward, Orr was thankful the evangelist ignored his advice, even as Orr questioned whether revival had fully erupted.

"It would be wrong to imagine that anyone claims that Southern California is experiencing anything like the Welsh Revival," Orr admitted.

The Graham meetings have a touch of revival in them along with the soulwinning, but they are more like the Torrey campaigns than the Welsh Revival. I am of the opinion that the work of God has advanced one step forward, and that the tide is rising on the Pacific Coast.... It is about time some good people made a choice between their sterile, faith-destroying, eschatological pessimism and the optimism which springs from the sure knowledge that God will revive His work in the midst of the years preceding the Coming, despite apostasy and because of it.[10]

Under Orr's influence, Graham looked to the era of Wesley and Whitefield and told the Los Angeles crowds how revival leads to social reform. When the meetings ran so long that the young preacher ran out of material, Graham reached back to this awakening for help from the most famous sermon ever preached on American soil, "Sinners in the Hands of an Angry God" by Jonathan Edwards. Graham adapted it for his own purposes, but the message flopped. Even so, the meetings were regarded as a rousing success.

Famed *Old-Fashioned Revival Hour* radio host Charles Fuller noted how so many had prayed so long for God to send a genuine revival. Now Fuller and his fellow evangelicals in Southern California had seen a glimpse of revival for themselves. But the revival wasn't confined to one region or even one country, Fuller learned. "Reports are coming to us from other parts of the world of a similar working of the Holy Spirit in convicting and converting power," he wrote to Ockenga. "Let us praise God and pray on for revival to spread throughout the length and breadth of our land, for surely His coming draweth nigh."[11]

Like Fuller, many who had long prayed for revival invested their hopes in Graham. Practically overnight, the talented Youth for Christ evangelist and Northwestern School president became an international sensation. "Everywhere we turned, someone wanted us to come and do for them what had been done in Los Angeles," Graham said. "What they didn't know, however, was that *we* had not done it. I was still a country preacher with too much on my plate. Whatever this could be called and whatever it would become, it was *God's* doing."[12]

Another Surprising Work of God

By contemporary accounts, God would do an even greater work of revival at the end of 1940 into 1950. Several of Ockenga's friends, including Fuller and Allan Emery Jr., a member of Park Street Church and prominent Boston businessman, suggested that he should invite Graham to New England. Ockenga wasn't immediately keen on the idea. The young dynamo with Hollywood good looks might impress Los Angeles, but in Boston they expected sophistication. There would be no testimonies from cowboy radio

Harold John Ockenga (left) initially resisted the idea of inviting Billy Graham (middle) to preach in sophisticated Boston. (Courtesy of the Archives of the Billy Graham Center, Wheaton, Illinois.)

hosts to boost Graham's cause in Boston. Plus, Ockenga had dreamed for years that God would allow *him* to be the catalyst for revival in New England, just like the olden days. Would the cultured Ph.D. pastor step aside for a North Carolina country boy?

In the end, Ockenga extended the invitation and Graham accepted. Unlike in Los Angeles, they had little time to prepare. They planned a New Year's Eve youth rally in Mechanics Hall, which could seat 6,000. That evening, they could not find nearly enough room for the crowds that turned out for the four-hour meeting. The next morning, the *Boston Post* reported how Ockenga had ended the meeting. He explained that the mid-century marked the beginning of a new era in human history. He spoke at the outset of a cold war on the heels of two world wars that claimed tens of millions of soldiers and citizens alike. The Soviet Union had tested their first nuclear weapon in August. But Ockenga told the youth that "millions of Americans believe an old-fashioned spiritual revival could preserve our God-given freedoms of and way of life."

He compared that evening to the "surprising work of God" in 1734 made famous by Edwards in Northampton, Massachusetts.[13]

Indeed, during the next two weeks in Boston, Graham preached for 115,000. About 3,000 of them professed decisions for Christ.[14] Favorable media coverage astounded longtime Bostonians. None other than the Roman Catholic diocese's newspaper said, "Bravo, Billy!" in an editorial. Ockenga's own church, among many congregations that sponsored the meetings, added more than 160 new members in just three months. Typically, Park Street Church welcomed 150 new members each year.[15] Ockenga related the thrilling events with vivid detail to the growing evangelical network around the country.

> Picture the largest halls in Boston such as the Opera House, the Mechanics Hall, and the Boston Garden, crowded to capacity, with people from every walk of life. Imagine that you can hear the swell of from six to fourteen thousand voices rising in old gospel choruses, evangelistic hymns and revival music. Behold the handsome, youthful, dynamic, fearless prophet declare the age old gospel as it is revealed in the Word of God. Watch the scores and scores of people responding to the invitation as they walk to the front and then enter an inquiry room where they are dealt with by personal workers. Listen as you ride in the buses, as you shop in the stores or visit the places of business where the name on everyone's tongue is Billy Graham and the Mid-Century Evangelistic Campaign, and you will have some idea of what is happening in Boston.[16]

Ockenga admitted it was hard to believe that such an awakening could stir Boston, a religious mixture of Roman Catholics, Christian Scientists, Unitarians, and modernists. The only explanation was that God had come to town, just as he was visiting other locales around the country. "We call the entire Christian public of the nation to prayer," Ockenga pleaded, "for if Boston and New England can receive such a shaking of God under this stripling who like David of old went forth to meet the giant of the enemy, then we believe that God is ready to shake America to its foundations in revival."[17]

Graham left Boston for a time to meet prior commitments, but he returned in March and April. Over five weeks, Graham visited twenty cities in all six New England states. Once again, the media adored him. From these press accounts, Garth Rosell identifies five characteristics they appreciated: "his winsome personality, his personal integrity, his commitment to moral purity, his biblical preaching, and his 'unction' from God."[18] These traits stemmed in part from commitment to the so-called Modesto Manifesto, a list of resolutions that Graham and his friends drew up in 1948. These guidelines were meant to protect them from the pitfalls of money, sex, and power that had claimed so many evangelists before them.

Not everyone adored Graham, though. Boston had been home to some of the First Great Awakening's most vocal critics. Continuing that legacy in the mid-twentieth century, several pastors spoke out against the religious fervor. "Some extreme liberal and Unitarian clergy said I was setting back the cause of religion a hundred years," Graham said. "I replied that I did indeed want to set religion back—not just a hundred years but nineteen hundred years, to the Book of Acts, where first-century followers of Christ were accused of turning the Roman Empire upside down."[19]

Graham might not have turned America upside down, but he presided over events unseen for more than two centuries. The Boston events met Graham's four conditions for revival: repentance, prayer, church unity, and obedience to Scripture.[20] The Boston sphere of the revival culminated on April 23, 1950, when 50,000 braved dreary, 46-degree weather to hear Graham on the Boston Common. The location was Ockenga's idea. Graham spoke in the same common where Whitefield had addressed 23,000 without amplification in 1740.

"This has been an age in which we have humanized God and deified man, and we have worshiped at the throne of science," Graham told the crowd. "We thought that science could bring about Utopia. We must have a spiritual awakening similar to that which we had under Wesley and Whitefield."[21]

Indeed, the surprising response from throngs on both coasts convinced Graham and his colleagues that America was ripe for a spiritual harvest. "The euphoria of military victories in Europe and the Far East should have left most of us feeling self-sufficient and optimistic—hardly the ideal climate for a religious revival," Graham remembered.

> But instead, we were headed for anxiety and apathy. For one thing, we worried about a mushroom cloud drifting on the horizon of history over the ghost cities of Japan, and about a red star rising in Eastern Europe. Under this double threat to our security and happiness, what purpose was left in life? We didn't seem to have either an exhilarating sense of national destiny or a satisfying sense of personal identity....
>
> What we saw in 1950 were the stirrings of a wide-reaching spiritual search—stirrings that helped to create an unaccustomed audience for the Gospel. Disillusioned and disconnected people seemed willing to try anything. It was a morally promising but exceedingly perilous time.[22]

Graham's perspective was backed by sociologist Will Herberg, who published the book *Protestant-Catholic-Jew: An Essay in American Religion Sociology* in 1955. "That there has in recent years been an upswing of religion in the United States can hardly be doubted; the evidence is diverse, converging, and unequivocal beyond all possibilities of error," Herberg wrote.[23] Public opinion unexpectedly swung behind religion after World War II. Herberg observed that Clarence Darrow, such a menacing figure for believers during the early twentieth century, left behind no successor. No one of similar stature stepped forward to continue his iconoclastic cause.

Statistics reflected the shift. Between 1926 and 1950, while the U.S. population grew 28.6 percent, membership in religious bodies spiked 59.8 percent. Protestants grew most rapidly at 63.7 percent. The Baptist subset doubled. In only eight years, between 1950 and 1958, church membership grew from 57 percent of America's population to an all-time high of 63 percent.[24] In just five years, between 1947 and 1952, Bible sales doubled.[25]

Herberg also shared Graham's sense of America's "total insecurity" and a "crisis of Western civilization." He wrote, "The utter predicament of human existence is no longer simply a philosophical or theological proposition; it is the most patent of everyday facts. The hydrogen bomb, on which our survival depends, yet which threatens us with destruction, is the sinister symbol of our plight."[26]

Against this ominous backdrop, revivals cropped up in cities nationwide in 1950. Merv Rosell led massive meetings in Kansas City, where 250,000 turned out in a little more than three weeks. Iowa Governor William S. Beardsley granted Rosell permission to hold tent meetings in Des Moines on the state capitol lawn. Later that year, a Chicago evangelist pitched a tent at the Iowa State Fair. "This is a momentous occasion in the history of Iowa," Governor Beardsley announced to a crowd of 30,000. "We have been thrilled to have these meetings and to see all denominations across the state join in this endeavor for Christ. Spiritual revival is the greatest need in Iowa and throughout the world today. We will do all in our power to help in this Crusade for Christ. We urge the people of this state to seek God in this crisis hour."[27]

Such overt support from media and politicians convinced evangelicals like Ockenga that "America's hour has struck." He confidently predicted:

> I believe that 1950 will go down in history as the year of heaven-sent revival. God is sending the revival for which His remnant all through America — the true Bible-believing Christians who never bowed their knees to the Baal and Ashtoreth of Modernism or Secularism — have been praying. God is moving as He has not moved in America at least for four decades and as He has not moved in New England for two centuries.... You do not have to wait till next year. You don't have to wait ten years. You don't have to pray anymore, "Lord, send a revival." The revival is here![28]

Ockenga did not want to diminish the importance of steady, faithful gospel ministry. But he believed the times demanded a more dramatic movement of the Holy Spirit. Ockenga understood they were seeing just such an awakening in 1950. By God's grace, perhaps the revival would continue to grow.

Beloved, this is revival. Have you ever seen revival? You prayed for it. I prayed for it for twenty-five years. Now revival is here and what has happened out in Los Angeles and up in Boston can happen in every city of America today. I thank God for all the wonderful movements that have in past years been bringing souls to Christ. I would die if we did not have people saved at my church every Sunday. If we did not have people going into the mission fields; if we did not have young men going out in the ministry; if we were not supporting scores and scores of new missionaries all the time, I think I would leave the church. I couldn't stand it! However that may be, even though we have had the mercy drops falling around about us everywhere, the time is come when we need the showers; when we need the outpouring; when we need the windows of heaven to be opened; when we need the tides of sin that are coming in inundating this land to be rolled back to be held back by the likes of God. And God says He is looking everywhere for men whose hearts are perfect toward Him to do this job. "Where are the men that will do this thing in this hour?"[29]

Campus Crusader for Christ

Back in California, one such ambitious man prepared to assume his role as instigator of a global missionary movement. Today, Campus Crusade for Christ is the largest evangelical parachurch ministry not devoted to philanthropy. But this multifaceted student ministry wasn't even a gleam in Bill Bright's eye when he moved to Southern California in 1944. The Oklahoman migrated west searching for acting gigs, which he hoped would lead to a political career. Around Los Angeles, Bright began rubbing shoulders with a group who would become the most prominent evangelicals in the country. His friends included Dawson Trotman, who launched the Navigators ministry to sailors in 1933, and Charles Fuller, the radio evangelist who would found Fuller Theological Seminary in Pasadena.

Bright didn't find much luck acting, but he knew how to make money. Bright's Brandied Foods enabled the entrepreneur to enjoy the Hollywood lifestyle. His landlords invited him to the church of the rich and famous, First Presbyterian of Hollywood, at the time America's biggest Presbyterian congregation. Here he came under the influence of Henrietta Mears, who would eventually invite Bright and his wife, Vonette, to live with her. Teaching one night in the College Department about the apostle Paul's conversion on the Damascus road, Mears encouraged the young Christians to kneel and pray like Paul did: "Lord, what wilt Thou have me to do?" At home, Bright did as he was told. Suddenly he cared more about God than money. At this key turning point, Mears encouraged Bright to attend Princeton Seminary, where he matriculated in 1946. But with his business floundering back in Southern California, and with his Greek and Hebrew flagging, Bright suspended his studies and headed back west.

Following the war, as American GIs returned home, Mears was moved by the world's great need for Christ. She toured Europe in 1947 and saw the devastation for herself. Though the war had ended, modern philosophies continued to march against the gospel. Who would rise up to meet this challenge? "Meditating on the challenge that Mordecai gave to Esther, Mears believed that she and her Hollywood collegians had 'come to the kingdom for such a time as this,'" historian John Turner writes. "Reflecting the influence of Keswick spirituality, which emphasized 'absolute surrender' and the subsequent empowerment of the Holy Spirit, Mears urged her listeners to fully commit themselves to Jesus Christ and pray for divine wisdom to discern if God was calling them to mission work either overseas or at home."[30]

Once again, Bright responded to Mears's call to be "expendable for Christ." The same night that Mears delivered this impassioned appeal, she retired to her cabin along with Bright, Louis Evans Jr., son of the Hollywood Presbyterian pastor, and future U.S. Senate chaplain Richard Halverson. After praying and conversing, "we were overwhelmed with the presence of God," Bright later wrote about the beginning of the Fellowship of the Burning Heart. The small group borrowed the name from John Calvin's seal of a heart offered by an open hand. "It was one of those things I had never experienced, and I didn't know what to do. I just got on my knees and began to praise the Lord.... While we were all carried away with the sense of the holy presence of God, our minds were racing with creative ideas."[31]

Evans, Bright, and Halverson committed to read the Bible and pray for an hour every day, live a life of self-denial and self-discipline, share the good news whenever possible, and present themselves as living sacrifices fully consecrated to Christ.[32] Bright decided to resume his theological education and enrolled with the first class at Fuller Theological Seminary, led by seminary president Ockenga, who commuted from Boston. But Bright would not allow academic responsibilities to cut into time set aside for evangelism. He recruited seminary students and Hollywood Presbyterian members to evangelize the local universities, including USC and UCLA. Fuller faculty such as Carl F. H. Henry were pleased to learn about Bright's activities, including news that he and a colleague had helped lead the UCLA student body president to Christ.

Bill Bright (right) felt "great communion of spirit" with fellow evangelist Billy Graham. (Courtesy of the Archives of the Billy Graham Center, Wheaton, Illinois.)

Yet as with Princeton, Bright itched to work on the front lines more than he pined for time to hone his knowledge of ancient languages. He continued to seek audiences in local dormitories and fraternities. He was inspired by the talk Graham was so reluctant to give amid his crisis of biblical confidence at the 1949 College Briefing Conference. Bright went so far as to depict the time as an "extraordinary student awakening."

"I feel a great communion of spirit with him," Bright said about the soon-to-be-famous evangelist, "because it was here the Lord spoke to many of us, giving a new challenge for service plus a greater sense of urgency for the lost."[33] Orr, always on the lookout for revival, wrote, "The Lord was there in power, and not only was there repentance, private and public confession, restoration, and thorough revival, but conversions of the most unhopeful sinners occurred every day."[34]

Bright languished at Fuller until he finally withdrew for good in 1951. Looking to launch an official college ministry, Bright consulted several mentors, including Mears and his favorite Fuller professor, Wilbur Smith, who recommended the name Campus Crusade for Christ. Doubting churches would mobilize to evangelize and disciple these masses, Bright launched Crusade without denominational assistance. Bright was the right man in the right place at the right time. Southern California brimmed with revival fervor. Bright's idea coincided with dramatic changes in American education following World War II. Thanks to the GI Bill, more than 2 million veterans received a break on the costs of advanced education. In the four years after the war concluded, an additional 1 million Americans moved onto college campuses. "Campus Crusade's early years at UCLA coincided with a nationwide upsurge in campus religiosity parallel to the more general religious boom of the postwar years," Turner writes. "Across the United States, university officials pointed to thriving denominational ministries, the establishment of academic courses in religion, and the success of 'religious emphasis' weeks as evidence of Christianity's vitality."[35]

Backed by this favorable wind, Bright went to work introducing UCLA campus leaders to the gospel. Bright found much more success in the Greek system than he did with Greek syntax. Speaking at the Kappa Alpha Theta sorority, Bright met Marilyn Amende and her boyfriend, Donn Moomaw, an All-American football player. Like many others Crusade would reach, Moomaw had grown up attending a mainline Protestant church but no longer bothered once he enrolled at UCLA. In a succinct process that he would codify as the Four Spiritual Laws, Bright talked Moomaw through several passages of Scripture, including Romans 3:23 and 6:23, and invited him to confess his sin and receive Christ as Savior. On the spot, the evangelist and linebacker kneeled together and prayed. Moomaw later passed up his chance to play in the NFL to study at Princeton Seminary. Bright and Moomaw left a deep gospel impression on the team. When UCLA won the national championship in 1954, the team was nicknamed the "Eleven from Heaven."

A strong partner and dynamic evangelist in her own right, Vonette joined Bill in campus ministry. In their first semester working on the UCLA campus, she led more than fifty women to Christ. Overall, more than 250 UCLA students professed faith in Christ during the ministry's first few months.[36] According to the Brights' vision of national and international expansion, Crusade grew to thirty staff members by 1955. Seeking resources for how to help these converts grow in their faith, several Crusade staff turned to Trotman's Navigators ministry for help. Trotman had likewise assisted Billy Graham when evangelistic success bumped up against parachurch limitations. InterVarsity had already been active on several American campuses since 1941, a decade before Crusade began popping up at UCLA and elsewhere. But InterVarsity shared Crusade's evangelical commitments and dubbed the 1950–51 school year "The Year of Evangelism." The campus ministries didn't always see eye to eye in their methodology. But they each stepped into a void left by denominational decline and met the spiritual needs of a generation returning from war and searching for meaning.

In the wake of denominational disputes and disarray, it is no surprise the new wave of evangelical fervor favored parachurch ministries. Orr recognized this difference from previous revivals as a threat to the resurgent movement's vitality and longevity. Though evangelical influence shifted toward parachurch ministries, leaders could not avoid old problems related to ecumenical compromise. The big tent wasn't big enough for fundamentalists who objected to Graham partnering with the liberal Protestant Council for his watershed New York Crusade in 1957. Graham reached even greater heights of national fame and approval, but evangelicals and fundamentalists retreated into sparring camps.

Despite this setback, the revivals of the late 1940s and early 1950s carved out space for a vibrant, diverse evangelical movement that survives today. Still dependent on parachurch publishing houses, schools, and missions agencies, evangelicals have now also invested heavily in local churches and networks that support them. The recent church-planting boom reveals how evangelical priorities have shifted. In these new churches, evangelicals seek to embody the traits evidenced in revival, including repentance, prayer, worship, unity, evangelism, and biblical preaching. Like their mid-century forerunners, today's evangelicals recognize that an unbelieving world takes notice of a church set apart for God and his glory.

"The evangelical task primarily is the preaching of the Gospel, in the interest of individual regeneration by the supernatural grace of God, in such a way that divine redemption can be recognized as the best solution of our problems, individual and social," Carl Henry wrote in his landmark 1947 book, *The Uneasy Conscience of Modern Fundamentalism.*

This produces within history, through the regenerative work of the Holy Spirit, a divine society that transcends national and international lines. The corporate testimony of believers, in their purity of life, should provide for the world an example of the divine dynamic to overcome evils in every realm. The social problems of our day are much more complex than in apostolic times, but they do not on that account differ in principle. When the twentieth century church begins to "out-live" its environment as the first century church outreached its pagan neighbors, the modern mind, too, will stop casting about for other solutions.[37]

NOTES

1. H. J. Ockenga, "The Hope for a Revival," *United Evangelical Action* (September 1, 1942), 4.

2. Garth M. Rosell, *The Surprising Work of God: Harold John Ockenga, Billy Graham, and the Rebirth of Evangelicalism* (Grand Rapids: Baker, 2008), 113–14.

3. Ibid., 111.

4. J. Edwin Orr, *The Second Evangelical Awakening in America* (London: Marshall, Logan & Scott, 1952), 190.

5. Billy Graham, *Just as I Am* (New York: HarperSanFrancisco: 1997), 138–39.

6. Joel A. Carpenter, *Revive Us Again: The Reawakening of American Fundamentalism* (New York: Oxford University Press, 1997), 217.

7. J. Edwin Orr, *Good News in Bad Times: Signs of Revival* (Grand Rapids: Zondervan, 1953), 42–43.

8. Billy Graham, "We Need Revival," in *Revival in Our Time: The Story of the Billy Graham Evangelistic Campaigns Including Six of His Sermons* (Wheaton, Ill.: Van Kampen Press, 1950), 70.

9. Mel Larson, "Tasting Revival," in *Revival in Our Time: The Story of the Billy Graham Evangelistic Campaigns Including Six of His Sermons* (Wheaton, Ill.: Van Kampen Press, 1950), 18–19.

10. J. Edwin Orr, "The Tide Is Rising in Southern California: Prayer, Consecration, Revival," *United Evangelical Action* (December 1, 1949), 12.

11. Rosell, *Surprising Work of God*, 131.

12. Graham, *Just as I Am*, 158.

13. Rosell, *Surprising Work of God*, 38.

14. Ibid., 139.

15. Jerry Beavan, "New England Revival—Second Phase," in *Revival in Our Time: The Story of the Billy Graham Evangelistic Campaigns Including Six of His Sermons* (Wheaton, Ill.: Van Kampen Press, 1950), 53.

16. Harold J. Ockenga, "Boston Stirred by Revival," *United Evangelical Action* (January 15, 1950), 4.

17. Ibid.

18. Rosell, *Surprising Work of God*, 141.

19. Graham, *Just as I Am*, 160.

20. Rosell, *Surprising Work of God*, 135.

21. Graham, *Just as I Am*, 168.

22. Ibid., 170–71.

23. Will Herberg, *Protestant-Catholic-Jew: An Essay in American Religion Sociology*, 2nd ed. (Garden City, N.Y: Anchor Books, 1960), 56.

24. Ibid., 47.

25. Carpenter, *Revive Us Again*, 213.

26. Herberg, *Protestant-Catholic-Jew*, 60.

27. Orr, *Good News in Bad Times*, 180.

28. Harold John Ockenga, "Is America's Revival Breaking?" *United Evangelical Action* (July 1, 1950), 3.

29. Ibid., 4.

30. John G. Turner, *Bill Bright and Campus Crusade for Christ: The Renewal of Evangelicalism in Postwar America* (Chapel Hill: University of North Carolina Press, 2008), 26.

31. Michael Richardson, *Amazing Faith: The Authorized Biography of Bill Bright* (Colorado Springs: Waterbrook, 2000), 36–37.

32. Ibid., 38.

33. Orr, *Second Evangelical Awakening in America*, 190.

34. Orr, "Tide Is Rising in Southern California," 3.

35. Turner, *Bill Bright and Campus Crusade for Christ*, 45.

36. Richardson, *Amazing Faith*, 65.

37. Carl F. H. Henry, *The Uneasy Conscience of Modern Fundamentalism* (Grand Rapids: Eerdmans, 1947), 88–89.

A GOD-SIZED VISION

In this tour of revival stories, we've seen how a diverse cast of men and women with a "God-sized vision" have been used as catalysts for true, divinely inspired awakenings. Whatever else you might say about Jonathan Edwards, he certainly heads the list with an especially "God-sized vision" of spiritual awakenings. As he studied Scripture, Edwards saw how God acts with sovereign grace and awesome power. But Edwards's vision was also shaped and strengthened by experience. His *Narrative of the Surprising Work of the Spirit of God*, published in 1737, described an amazing event. Northampton, Massachusetts, and neighboring towns in the Connecticut River Valley had been blessed by "a special dispensation of God's providence." The townspeople recognized the very "presence of the Lord" in their midst. According to Edwards, God's presence transformed the spiritual life of the town. After laboring faithfully for years without spectacular results, Edwards marveled at how rapidly the work of the Lord advanced.

"When God in so remarkable a manner took the work in his own hands, there was as much done in a day or two, as at ordinary times, with all the endeavors that men can use, and with such a blessing as we commonly have, is done in a year."[1]

Edwards rejoiced as the work of the Holy Spirit swept beyond the Northampton town limits. But Edwards did not attribute the spread of the awakening to any planning by the New England clergy. Rather, he regarded the revival as surprising, even though he and other ministers had seen revival before and prayed for it expectantly. Edwards's account provides us with a vivid example of how the Lord transforms individual lives and entire communities. This revival story, along with the many others already recounted in this volume, may in turn stretch our vision of God's powerful and gracious work in the past. The stories may also stir us to pray that God will pour out his Holy Spirit once again in great power in our own day.

Yet maybe you remain unconvinced. We don't see revivals like this in the West today. Most of us have never participated in a major spiritual awakening. So we may conclude that they simply do not happen, at least not where we live. Our experience (or lack thereof) trumps biblical teaching and historical example. What is more, few evangelical leaders call on us to remember the reviving work of the Spirit of God in our land. Where are the voices crying out in the wilderness, imploring the children of Israel to remember God's prior acts of faithfulness and power?

Centuries ago, the Protestant Reformer John Calvin observed that we have a strong bent to elevate the knowledge of man above the knowledge of God. For Calvin, viewing the world according to man's knowledge alone leads to great spiritual loss. Out attempts to understand life essentially based on what we have experienced or on what we see in the culture can genuinely hinder us from seeing reality from God's point of view. According to Calvin, we cannot really understand who we are unless we first have knowledge of God, an understanding of God and his standards of righteousness. Using experience alone as a judge badly clouds our vision, especially as it relates to our salvation and self-understanding.

"So long as we do not look beyond the earth, we are quite pleased with our own righteousness, wisdom, and virtue; we address ourselves in the most flattering terms, and seem only less than demigods," Calvin wrote.

> But should we once begin to raise our thoughts to God, and reflect what kind of Being he is, and how absolute the perfection of that righteousness, and wisdom, and virtue, to which,

as a standard, we are bound to be conformed, what formerly delighted us by its false show of righteousness will become polluted with the greatest iniquity; what strangely imposed upon us under the name of wisdom will disgust by its extreme folly; and what presented the appearance of virtuous energy will be condemned as the most miserable impotence.[2]

For Calvin, then, a God-sized vision constitutes far more than having a "big" vision of God's capacity to display great power in the world. Rather, it calls us to completely reorient our frame of reference through which we look at the world. Someone who lives with a God-sized vision affirms that gaining knowledge of God precedes gaining knowledge of man. To acquire this knowledge of God, we turn to Scripture. There we see Christ, and in reflecting on Christ, we gain more knowledge of God the Father. As Martin Luther observes, Christ is a mirror of our heavenly Father's loving heart.

Yet this Father will also judge according to his own standards of righteousness, not ours. This God holds the nations in his hands. He alone empowers our ministry. We must not depend on methods, cultural exegesis, strategies, and techniques (helpful though some of them can be) as our end-all approach to doing ministry. We desperately need to depend on the power of the Holy Spirit in our day-to-day lives. A God-sized vision helps us to understand that the Lord really does love us and care for us. He provides for us. The doctrine of God's providence gives us both courage and comfort. Trusting that God as our loving heavenly Father wants our good, we can even dare to pray the Lord's Prayer with sincerity, including the phrase "Thy will be done."

The stories recounted in this volume demonstrate the God-sized vision in action. Yet perhaps your doubts persist. Haven't historians found ways of explaining this religious fervor? How do we know we can trust these accounts as something more than the result of overheated imaginations and naive misreadings of religious phenomena? Such questions are not new to our day. Edwards foresaw that critics would charge him with fabricating fanciful and exaggerated claims. Like his friend George Whitefield, Edwards determined he could not remain silent about what he had witnessed or heard about through reliable sources. He feared that if he did not testify publicly to God's role in the awakening, he would be robbing the Lord of his glory.

> I am very sensible how apt many would be if they should see the account I have here given, presently to think with themselves that I am very fond of making a great many converts, and of magnifying and aggrandizing the matter; and to think that, for want of judgment, I take every religious pang, and enthusiastic conceit, for saving conversion; and I don't much wonder if they should be apt to think so; … but having now as I thought a special call to give an account of it upon mature consideration I thought it might not be beside my duty to declare this amazing work, as it appeared to me, to be indeed divine, and to conceal no part of the glory of it, leaving with God to take care of the credit of his own work, and running the venture of any censorious thoughts which might be entertained of me to my disadvantage.[3]

Still, sincerity can only take us so far. How do we evaluate the many claims of revival we hear today from around the world? Edwards did not support everything he heard about in connection with the revival that became known as the Great Awakening. He contributed a set of criteria for discerning a true work of God that helped us write this book. According to Edwards, a true revival exalts Jesus Christ, provokes Satan, prioritizes the Bible, and inspires love. But there are other traits these revival stories share in common. If we will see revival again in this day of diminished expectations, we would expect to hear about these shared traits that can be traced throughout the history of spiritual awakenings.

Persisting in Prayer

Often, at least a handful of faith-filled believers engaged in heartfelt prayer for an outpouring of the Holy Spirit in order to experience revival. Sometimes they prayed for years before they saw revival. Others were driven to pray almost as a last resort. They had tried and failed to do ministry in their own power. They realized the task before them was too huge or that their efforts using various means and methods had failed. They finally acknowledged they could not continue to serve without the Lord's blessing and power.

Edwards saw a direct connection between prayer and spiritual awakenings. He noted that the church gave itself to prayer before God poured out his Spirit on Jerusalem. Edwards's grandson Timothy Dwight implored the Lord to move in power upon the students of Yale College. James McGready and others bound themselves in 1797 to an oath to pray regularly for sinners in spiritually deadened Logan County, Kentucky. Jeremiah Lanphier invited New Yorkers off the street to join him in prayer. Evan Roberts prayed for eleven years before the Welsh revival broke out in 1905. Examples abound of faithful men and women, sometimes only two or three together, who gave themselves to incessant prayer for revival.

Repenting from Sin

When God's presence becomes evident in a revival, repentance from sin swiftly follows. The revivals in China and Korea illustrate this trait most vividly. Awareness of God's holiness impels believers under conviction of the Holy Spirit to seek Christ's forgiveness. Sin's horror becomes unbearably evident. The sin could be as simple and insidious as pride and trust in our own efforts. But God could be waiting for us to confess before he reveals his plans. There is a danger, however. Sometimes public confession becomes a twisted sort of spiritual one-upmanship to see who can reveal the worst sin. Several recent college revivals have been plagued by this problem. Confession must be followed by humble pursuit of God's sustaining grace and ongoing accountability. But make no mistake, true revival will expose sin you never noticed. The process will be bitter, but God's grace will soon taste sweeter than ever before.

Preaching the Gospel of Jesus Christ

During the transatlantic awakening of the eighteenth century, John Wesley, George Whitefield, and Jonathan Edwards preached the gospel of Jesus Christ to whoever would listen, whether in churches, open fields, or town squares. Empowered by the Holy Spirit, their preaching breached man-made defenses. They emphasized the doctrine of justification by faith alone, which they believed had been lost in much Anglican preaching of their day. They understood that the gospel is "the power of God unto salvation" (Rom. 1:16). Reformation and revival need not compete.[4] We need pastors who will teach the faith once delivered to the saints and evangelists who will communicate it passionately and clearly. Reformation might be just the thing that recovers the gospel in our churches and unleashes the power of God to stir the affections. Indeed, if reform does not accompany revival, the awakening will dissipate with fanaticism.

Acknowledging God's Authority in Humility

Christians throughout history have emphasized the importance of walking humbly before God and neighbors. Edwards noted that humility not only helps to keep the Devil at bay, but also clears one's vision. He knew that the Lord often used humble believers to lead spiritual awakenings. Gripped by the gospel, they exalted Christ and not themselves.

By contrast, Edwards identified pride as the primary error that clogged the advance of awakenings. Pride, a stubborn enemy of God, was the first sin that came into this world and will be the last one to leave. Those who are eager to see the gospel advance are particularly prone to pride. A humble person whom God chose to use in ministry could become proud about success and popularity, succumb to a critical spirit, and in turn lose the Lord's full blessing. Edwards's insights on spiritual pride in particular deserve serious consideration.

> Spiritual pride is very apt to suspect others; whereas an humble saint is most jealous of himself, he is so suspicious of nothing in the world as he is of his own heart. The spiritually proud person is apt to find fault with other saints, that they are low in grace, and to be much in observing how cold and dead

they be, and crying out of them for it, and to be quick to discern and take notice of their deficiencies: but the eminently humble Christian has so much to do at home, and sees so much evil in his own heart, and is so concerned about it, that he is not apt to be very busy with others' hearts; he complains most of himself, and cries out of his own coldness and lowness in grace, and is apt to esteem others better than himself ... and can't bear to think that others should bring forth no more fruit to God's honor than he.[5]

A humble Christian is more apt to seek reconciliation with estranged brothers and sisters in Christ and to say in a heartfelt manner, "I am sorry." Reconciliation between antagonistic Christians often seems to open the door to revival. We recall that after Jonathan Goforth sought reconciliation with another missionary, even though Goforth felt he was in the right, revival broke out among the Chinese with whom he was ministering. Nursing personal grudges can diminish our fruitfulness in ministry.

When we are weak, God is strong. When God is strong, we worship. When we worship, the world notices. When God sends revival once more, the world won't be able to ignore it.

Serving God with Boldness

With a firm belief in God's care, many revival leaders fearlessly entered perilous circumstances. They were not content to serve as chaplains to the status quo. John Wesley found himself at the center of numerous riots; Jonathan Goforth narrowly escaped the Boxer uprising. This holy boldness, granted by the Spirit, gains strength when we remember what God's strong arm has done in the past. The Lord is not intimidated by Chicago or Cairo or any other city or country. He really does hold the nations in his hands. History tells the story. Nations rise and fall, but the Lord endures forever. Christ is building his church.

"This is what God can do. This is what God has done," Martyn Lloyd-Jones said. "Let us together decide to beseech him, to plead with him to do this again. Not that we may have the experience or the excitement, but that his mighty hand may be known and his great name may be glorified and magnified among the people."[6]

May we walk humbly before the Lord, confess our sins, give thanks for the salvation we have in Jesus Christ, and pray that God in his gracious kindness might pour out his Spirit, not only upon us or our churches, but upon the cities and nations of the world. The fledgling churches in Asia and Africa once found inspiration in stories of revival from the West. Now, as the global church grows deeper and wider, let us listen for their stories of God's grace and find inspiration to ask the heavenly Father for a special effusion of his Holy Spirit. We cannot fully comprehend the ways of God. But we can begin to develop a God-sized vision by recognizing the gap between our expectations and his promises, embedded in stories of his mighty acts, recorded in Scripture and continuing through the ages.

Though revival is supernatural, it is not magical. It does not solve all the church's problems. In fact, revival can create new ones as Satan counterattacks God's people. We do not intend to characterize revival as the solution to all the church's ills. Revival, in fact, looks a lot like the church's normal activities as explained in Scripture. The revived church worships, prays, preaches, and evangelizes. Only they do so with a heightened sense of God and greater capacity to embody and proclaim the good news of Jesus Christ's death and resurrection for sinners. Their Christ-centered exuberance in worship and boldness in evangelism attracts critics but appeals to many others. A deeper understanding of God's holiness leads to repentance and humility that may seem uncomfortable at first but ultimately foster meaningful community. In short, a true revival has erupted when the church together can see the Holy Spirit exalt God in his glory as revealed in Jesus Christ. We won't behold this scene in all its fullness until heaven. But every Christian can and should ask God to vindicate his name and demonstrate his glory by giving us a preview here and now.

NOTES

1. Jonathan Edwards, "A Faithful Narrative of the Surprising Work of God," in *A Jonathan Edwards Reader*, ed. John E. Smith, Harry S. Stout, and Kenneth P. Minkema (New Haven, Conn.: Yale University Press, 1995), 67.

2. John Calvin, *Institutes of the Christian Religion*, bk. 1, chap. 1, trans. Henry Beveridge (Grand Rapids: Eerdmans, 1989), 38–39.

3. Edwards, "Faithful Narrative of the Surprising Work of God," 67.

4. Richard F. Lovelace, *Dynamics of Spiritual Life: An Evangelical Theology of Renewal* (Downers Grove, Ill.: InterVarsity, 1979), 16.

5. Jonathan Edwards, *The Great Awakening*, vol. 4 of *The Works of Jonathan Edwards*, ed. C. C. Goen (New Haven, Conn.: Yale University Press, 1972), 418.

6. Martyn Lloyd-Jones, *Revival* (Wheaton, Ill.: Crossway, 1987), 117.

INDEX